A Guide to Chris

This is a book f
cover the lost contemplative dimension of
their Christian heritage. Most people will
accept Christ's words intellectually to "seek
the kingdom of God within," but they don't
know how to go about it. Here are specific
techniques. The writings of Christian mystics and spiritual leaders throughout history
are a rich mine of time-tested methods for
effective meditation, and Mrs. Helleberg
helps us to "take out the gold."

Marilyn Morgan Helleberg was born in
Nebraska and still lives there, writing and
teaching at Kearney State College. She is a
regular contributor to **Guideposts** magazine, is married and the mother of three
children.

A Guide to
Christian Meditation

A Guide to Christian Meditation

MARILYN MORGAN HELLEBERG

Phoenix Press

WALKER AND COMPANY
New York

Large Print Edition published by arrangement with Paulist Press

Acknowledgements

I wish to express my appreciation to **Guideposts** for granting
permission to reprint my article "Go Ahead, Hate Me!" (copyright
1977 by Guideposts Associates Inc.) which appeared in the August
1977 issue of that magazine. I am further grateful to **Guideposts** for
giving me permission to retell, in these pages, some of my personal
experiences that originally appeared in the volume **Daily Guideposts,
1979**; to Unity School of Christianity for allowing me to reprint poems
by Jim Rosemergy and Lowell Fillmore that appeared in the August
and November 1977 issues of **Unity** magazine; and to Richard Bowen,
whose poem, "Please Hear What I'm **Not** Saying," is reprinted from
the November 1977 issue of **The Chimes**.

All scriptural references are from the King James Version of the
Holy Bible.

My very special thanks to Anna, Norman, Vernon, and all the
others who have walked with me through secret places in the silent
Presence of the Holy One, and to David, who first opened the door.

Library of Congress Cataloging in Publication Data

Helleberg, Marilyn M.
  A guide to Christian meditation.

  Originally published: Beyond TM. New York : Paulist
Press, c1980.
  1. Meditation.   2. Large type books.   I. Title.
[BV4813.H38 1984]   248.3′4   84-15349
ISBN 0-8027-2489-2 (lg. print)

Printed in the United States of America

First Large Print Edition, 1984
Walker and Company
720 Fifth Avenue
New York, New York 10019

To Karen, Paul, and John,
my companions on this spiritual journey;
and to their father, Rex,
my companion for life.

Contents

Preface

MY little boy answered the phone the other day and said, "Mom's meditating right now. May I have her call you back in a few minutes?"

When I returned my friend's call, she was still in a state of shock. "Don't tell me you're into that *occult* stuff! You, of all people! Don't you realize meditation is *unchristian*?"

The unsettling thing is that my friend's reaction is not at all uncommon. But why should meditation be a dirty word for Christians? From the time that Jesus first went off by Himself into the wilderness, until now, devout Christians of all ages have been practicing the Presence of God through prayer and meditation.

And yet, I think many of us have neglected the contemplative part of our Christian heritage. We accept, intellectually at least, Christ's advice to seek the kingdom of God within, but *we don't know how to go about it*. We need specific techniques! The writings of Christian mystics and spiritual leaders throughout history are a rich mine of time-tested methods for effective meditation, but to be honest, it's sometimes kind of hard to dig out the gold. Most of us simply don't have the time nor the inclination to pursue these rather abstruse sources. That's why I asked for a leave of absence from my college classes so that I could do some mining for you. In addition to the writings of others, I have also mined my inner self through my own Christ-centered meditation; and most important of all, I have tried to stay open to the inner voice of God. If there are any treasures in this book you may be sure they came from Him and not from me.

I hope you will find this book both practical and inspirational. It includes specific techniques for meditation, all with a Christian emphasis, that will help you to find the kingdom of God that is within you. Beyond that, it gives down-to-earth methods for coping with the problems of daily living with the help of meditation.

Each chapter includes not only a discussion of techniques for practical results, but also one or more guided meditations designed to lead you into deeper and deeper levels of Christ-consciousness. In the beginning these guided meditations may seem to be mere fantasy, but you will soon become aware of a deep sense of validity in the experiences. This is because they put you in touch with a reality that transcends ordinary consciousness.

This is a heart-level, person-to-person book. In it, I have shared many of my own personal experiences with you because we walk the path together, you and I, and I, too, am trying to learn more about meditation and the spiritual journey. The style is informal because, as I wrote, I pictured you sitting in the chair by my desk, and I just wrote down the things I wanted to tell you.

The night I started writing the book a prayer came into my heart. I wrote it down, taped it on the wall above my desk, and carried it in my heart throughout the writing:

Lord Jesus Christ, in this moment and

for all eternity, I offer You my body, mind, heart, soul, and spirit, and dedicate to You whatever work You may want to do through me. Help me to be unerringly true to the inner voice—Your voice. I *expect* it (You) to surprise me with truths I didn't know I knew— truths that will inspire, uplift, and unify those who read them. Help me to let go of the ground of rigid rationality for the sake of the creative, intuitive leap that touches the hem of your garment. Help me to erase my little ego self in the vastness of Your message. Let *love* hover over the pages and come to nest, gently and warmly, in the spiritual hearts of those who read these words. Amen.

1

What is Christian Meditation?

THERE is a song that echoes in the hollows of the heart. There is a rhythm that waltzes in the shadows of the soul. There is a symphony that sings in the silence of the spirit. Somewhere, sometime, however faintly, *you* have heard the echo of that song, felt the rhythm of that waltz, sensed the surging of that symphony, or you would not have chosen this book.

I'm not sure when I first became aware of the mellow measured beat of that silent music within me. The first chords may have sounded in the heart of that solitary child swinging under the wisteria arbor in our back yard, or in the starry-eyed dreams of that painfully shy teen-ager, or in the miracle of that moment when a young mother first held her living, breathing baby girl in her arms.

Only now, looking back through the

1

web of my own doubts, fears, and misunderstandings about meditation, can I see that the music was always there, deep and organ-toned, waiting only for ears that could hear.

I resisted the idea of meditation at first because of the misguided notion that it might somehow be unchristian. But a thorough study of related scripture and inspirational literature, coupled with prayerful meditation in Christ's words, have shown me that I had nothing to fear. Whatever meditation may be to people of other religions, I discovered that, for me, the Composer, Conductor, and Musicians of that inner symphony were, in truth, Father, Son and Holy Spirit.

My own study of meditation techniques began as a search for a deeper awareness of the presence of Christ in my life. I earnestly wanted to learn to meditate, but I didn't want to join an Eastern religion in order to do it.

If you have doubts about whether or not meditation is really appropriate for Christians, maybe it will help if I share with you some of the misgivings I had when I first felt drawn to the idea of meditation.

Then I'd like to quote from a few of the sources that helped me to overcome my hesitation, in the hope that they will help you, as they did me.

If this chapter seems to get a big bogged down with quotations and explanations, let me assure you that we will very soon get to the practical business of *how* to meditate. But when we do begin, I want you to be able to put your *whole self* into it; so I hope the information in this chapter may help to free any parts of you that may be holding back a little.

So much has been written in the past few years about the meditation practices of Eastern religions that, for many Christians, the very word *meditation* conjures up visions of white-robed gurus sitting cross-legged on the floor counting beads. Because such things seem alien to many Westerners, they often close the doors of their minds and run. So I had to ask myself the question: *Is meditation REALLY for Christians, too?*

What does the Bible say?

I began to search the scriptures and found that there are many, many references to meditation. God Himself clearly *commands* it in the first chapter of Joshua: "This book of the law shall not depart out of your mouth, but you shall meditate on it day and night . . ." (Joshua 1:8). Clearly, God's command to Joshua involves more than just *reading* the scriptures. When you meditate on something "day and night," your knowledge of it passes beyond mere conscious, intellectual reasoning until it becomes a part of the very fabric of your soul. But there's another command of God's that comes closer to the kind of meditation I'm going to teach you. It's "Be still and know that I am God" (Psalms 46:10). What better definition of meditation could there possibly be?

As I read the other passages about meditation, *in context*, I discovered that, instead of the watered-down interpretation many moderns give to the word (to think seriously about a problem, for instance), meditation is a deeply spiritual and exciting practice that makes the meditator aware of the fact that he is in the very presence of the living God. It is food and water to the soul that hungers and thirsts: "O God, thou art my God; early will I seek thee, my flesh longeth for thee in a dry and thirsty land, where no water is; . . . My soul shall be satisfied as with marrow and fatness; and my mouth shall praise thee with joyful lips, when I remember thee upon my bed, and meditate on thee in the night watches" (Psalms 63:1 and 5).

Meditation, in the biblical context, is not merely an intellectual exercise; it is a *way of knowing* that is greater than mere knowledge of facts. "My mouth shall speak of *wisdom*; and the meditation of my heart shall be of *understanding*" (Psalms 49:3; italics added).

It is an inner gift that transforms lives. Psalm one speaks of the man whose "delight is in the law of the Lord; and in his law doth he meditate day and night. And he shall be like a tree planted by the rivers of water, that bringeth forth his fruit in his season; his leaf also shall not wither; and whatsoever he doeth shall prosper" (Psalms 1:1–3). These and many other passages of scripture convinced me that

God's Word endorses the idea of meditation.

Christian meditators of the past

Along with the study of scripture, I also began reading the lives and writings of great Christians, from early centuries to the present, and I found that devout Christians of all ages have practiced the presence of God through meditation.* We know that Jesus Himself withdrew from the multitudes periodically to commune with the Father through prayer and meditation. His example was followed by the author of the fourth gospel, St. John, and by St. Paul, who reached the heights of Christ-consciousness so that he was able to say: "I live; yet not I, but Christ liveth in me" (Galatians 2:20).

St. Augustine's *Confessions*, written in the last part of the fourth century, tell of the mystical formulas that were the basis of his intense spiritual experience; and the

---

*Some of the forms of meditation discussed in this book have been called contemplation or contemplative prayer by others.

6

hours that St. Francis of Assisi spent in contemplative communion with God transformed his life. Dante and Meister Eckhart, writers and scholars of the thirteenth and fourteenth centuries, combined mystical insight with intense intellectual power, and they were followed by the unknown author of *The Cloud of Unknowing*, who gave clear and direct instructions about Christian meditation:

> This is what you are to do: lift up your heart to the Lord, with a gentle stirring of love desiring him for his own sake and not for his gifts. Center all your attention and desire on him and let this be the sole concern of your mind and heart.

Christian meditation was well developed within the Byzantine Church, where it was known as Hesychasm. The method involved a form of repetitive prayer that was called "The Prayer of the Heart" or the "Jesus Prayer."

In the sixteenth Century, St. Teresa infused new vitality into the body of Christ with her stress on the importance of direct communion with God through meditation.

Her contemporary, the psychologist-philosopher-mystic known as St. John of the Cross, left a rich legacy of written guidance on Christian meditation. I especially like his description of meditation as "the privilege of listening for the delicate voice of God."

Christian meditation is not, however, restricted to Catholic saints. In its earlier stages, Luther's revolt was not aimed at destroying the Catholic religion, but at breaking up its rigid and petrifying emphasis on external forms, so that the spiritual possibilities of the inner man might be freed and expanded. John Wesley's great appeal was not concerned with new doctrine, but with the need for intimate personal experience between God and the individual man.

Jacob Boehme, a Lutheran of the late sixteenth and early seventeenth-century Protestant movement in Germany, wrote much about the meditative state. Among other noted Protestant mystics of the past are: George Fox, the founder of the Quakers, who taught his followers to listen for the "still small voice" within; Peter Poiret, a Protestant pastor who wrote about

Christian meditation in the late seventeenth and early eighteenth century; and William Blake, the English Protestant mystic whose prophetic writings rest on a personal and inward communion with God. There are many others but this is just a quick glimpse of a few of the Christian meditators of the past.

Modern writers on Christian meditation

Some of the twentieth-century writers about meditation who approach the subject from a Christian frame of reference include: Joel Goldsmith, William Johnston, Paul Tillich, George Maloney, M. Basil Pennington, Thomas R. Kelly, Morton T. Kelsey, among others. David S. Fetcho in an article for *His* magazine (November, 1977), gives us this piercing insight into Christian meditation:

At the core of Christ's atonement for our sin is a real supernatural exchange. Jesus Christ substitutes his life for ours. It is in the intimate proximity of that exchange that the Christian's meditation takes place. And it is the full resources of our humanity that we bring to the artistic act of meditation. By that act, we engage our lives with the redemptive work of grace, whereby we are conformed to the image of Christ.

I have given just a few broad strokes as a small sampling of the many, many Christians who have written about meditation experiences, but I think you can see why such readings soon dissolved all my doubts about whether or not meditation is appropriate for Christians. The exciting development that I see now is in the fact that, while meditation used to be pretty much confined to mystics, and saints, more and more everyday people, such as you and I, are feeling the need for the closer, more personal communion with Christ that meditation brings.

Still, there are some other questions that Christians who are considering meditation sometimes ask. If you are bothered by some of these questions, you deserve some carefully considered, objective answers.

Answers to your questions about Christian meditation

1. *Is meditation just a form of self-hypnosis?* This is a reasonable question because we sometimes give ourselves suggestions to help us relax as we're preparing for meditation. Also, there are some forms of meditation that involve repetition, as do some forms of self-hypnosis. However, meditation is a state of restful *alertness*, of *heightened* awareness, while hypnosis tends to *suppress* awareness. Furthermore, as Christopher Isherwood points out, "If it's nothing but auto-hypnosis, you'll soon find out. Hypnosis wouldn't give you any lasting results. It wouldn't give you the peace and understanding you're looking for." But we don't have to take someone else's word for it. Scientists have demonstrated, through the use of the EEG machine, which measures brain-wave patterns, that meditation and hypnosis are two distinctly different states. The meditation state is characterized by a slow, steady brain-wave pattern called protracted alpha. William Johnston tells of some of these laboratory tests and their results:

First of all, no one can now say that meditation and mysticism are nothing but forms of self-hypnosis. The fact is that the person in a hypnotic trance does not necessarily enter into protracted alpha at all. His brain rhythms are more or less like those of any waking working person.

While self-hypnosis is often an attempt to convince oneself of something that is not actually true, the Christian meditator seeks, above all else, that *Truth* which is revealed in Christ. Self-hypnosis is merely a mental exercise, while "meditation is not an intellectual activity but an increase in the over-all quality and depth of our total awareness" (Scott Crom, professor of philosophy, Beloit College).

2. *Is meditation escapism?* I think it's fair to say that it *could become* that. There's a lovely metaphor that compares meditation to a ship in which a human being can travel toward God. If meditation deteriorates into mere escapism, then that's a sure sign that the boat has sprung a leak! True Christian meditation should be a tuning *in* and not a

tuning out. Those who have reached the highest states of consciousness through meditation have always lived lives of greatest service to mankind.

Talk of altered states of consciousness, of interior senses, of ecstasy and the rest might give us the impression that meditators and mystics are divorced from reality—whereas the contrary is true. Gandhi, Martin Luther King, Dag Hammarskjold, Thomas Merton still speak to us of a mystical life integrated with service to men. And apart from these giants there are a host of unknown people who integrate mysticism with the humdrum waking consciousness and with daily living in community or family (William Johnston).

When you go mountain-climbing, you don't plan to *live* up on the peaks, away from the problems of daily life. You climb in order to get a broader perspective, a clearer view of the valleys and the plains. Meditation, too, is a way of climbing that opens for you a broader, truer perspective, enabling you to come back down to the plains of everyday life and live more consciously, creatively, and effectively. It is as if, with Peter, James, and John, we catch a glimpse of the transfigured Christ. In the moment of that mystical exchange, our lives, too, are transformed, but Christ always leads us back down from the mountain in order that we may do his work in the world.

3. *Is meditation self-centered?* It may seem that way, especially to people who don't understand what meditation is really about. Actually, there's a paradox involved here —a seeming contradiction: the meditator goes into the deepest levels of his inner self *only in order to transcend the self*. Once you have met the living Christ in that inner stillness, you begin to meet Him everywhere. Meditation becomes a bridge between the inner and the outer being, a way of bringing an awareness of God into everyday life. It is the very opposite of selfishness. Christ-centered meditation makes one less judgmental, more compassionate in one's relationship with others.

Ardis Whitman writes: "To be deprived of inwardness is even, in fact, to be deprived of a true outward life, for only the understanding found in the depths of the self can lead us directly through our own experience to the larger world of the experience of others."

"In deep solitude I find the gentleness with which I can love my brother," wrote Thomas Merton.

4. *Is meditation "vain repetition"?* This question stems, of course, from Jesus' instructions concerning prayer, in Matthew 6:7: "But when ye pray, use not vain repetitions, as the heathen do: for they think that they shall be heard for their much speaking." Since some forms of meditation do involve repetition, including the "Logos meditation" that I will describe in some parts of this book, this is a question that deserves careful thought.

Let's view these words in context by looking at the succeeding verse in Matthew: "Be not ye therefore like unto them: for your Father knoweth what things ye have need of, before ye ask him." Clearly, Jesus was referring to those who continually beg God for one thing and then another, asking for the same things over and over, as if the more "speaking" they do, the more chance they will have of being heard. This is the exact opposite of meditative prayer, which seeks to *silence* that self-centered monologue so that the *voice of the Lord* may be heard.

The word, *vain*, means either "meaningless" or "self-centered." In some *non-Christian* forms of meditation, the words used are sometimes meaningless to the meditator. Transcendental Meditation (TM), for instance, uses Sanskrit words as "mantras," and the meditator doesn't know the meaning of the words he uses. On the other hand, the words I use for Logos meditation are taken from scripture, very often from the words of Jesus Himself, and the meditator is asked to allow their *meaning* to penetrate his consciousness. Please understand that I am not *judging* TM in any way. I'm just pointing out an important difference between that system of meditation and the one I propose in this book.

Logos meditation has as its supreme purpose the goal of transcending the narrow, self-centered little personal ego in order to enter more fully into the presence of God. So Logos meditation is not "vain repetition" because it is neither meaningless nor self-centered.

Of course, it is not new to Christianity, either. As I mentioned earlier, the Jesus Prayer originated with the Hesychast movement in the early Eastern Church, and similar forms of meditation were used in other parts of the Christian body. To quote again that fourteenth-century English mystic who wrote *The Cloud of Unknowing*:

If you want to gather all your desire into one simple word that the mind can easily retain, choose a short word rather than a long one. A one syllable word such as "God" or "love" is best. But choose one that is meaningful to you. Then fix it in your mind so that it will remain there come what may. This word will be your defense in conflict and in peace. Use it to beat upon the cloud of darkness above you and subdue all distractions, consigning them to the cloud of forgetting beneath you. Should some thought go on annoying you, demanding to know what you are doing, answer with this one word alone.

The fact that repetitive prayer has been used for centuries as a means of stilling the "much-speaking" of the conscious mind attests to its effectiveness.

Of course, this is only one kind of meditation and only a *part* of your total meditation experience, but it *is* a valuable tool for "centering in" and stilling the restless mind. Johnston helps to bring it into perspective:

> In the Western mystical tradition as it evolved since the sixteenth century, it was usual to begin meditation with a certain amount of reasoning and thinking about the scriptures, about the life of Christ and so on. This was called "discursive prayer" and in time it was simplified to the process of repeating aspirations (this was technically called "affective prayer") and finally to the repetition of one aspiration and the entrance into intuitive silence. This last stage was called "the prayer of simplicity" or "the prayer of the heart" or "the prayer of simple regard" or "acquired contemplation."

But *why? What is the purpose of repetitive prayer?* Evelyn Underhill says it well: "These practices are easily justifiable, not that they have in themselves, as material gestures, any religious value at all, but because they bring about in us . . . a harmony that is a prerequisite for the life of the Spirit."

Maybe an analogy will make it clearer. Have you ever been in a large gathering of people where several conversations were going on at the same time? Let's say the one voice you're *really* trying to listen to is softer than the others. What a strain it is to try to hear that voice, with all the other voices interfering. If you have a CB radio, you may know what it's like to have people "walking all over" the voice you're listening for. Your muscles become tense, your nerves start feeling jangled, and it's hard to concentrate. We may not realize it, but all of us are carrying on disorganized conversations within ourselves all the time. When we sit down and try to center our thoughts on God, we find them racing in every direction. We may *start out* thinking about God or visualizing Christ, but before long, we find ourselves replaying the conversation we had with our spouse that morning, or planning the day's activities, or worrying about our child's report card, or wondering if we remembered to mail that letter, etc., etc. Our mind is bombarded, just as it is in the room with the competing conversations. All of this makes us tense and, obviously, interferes with our ability to enter into Christ-consciousness.

But when we start repeating a single, *meaningful* word or phrase—one with Christian spiritual significance—we can focus on that "Logos" so that distraction, in the form of irrelevant thoughts, are eliminated. It has a steadying, calming, stabilizing effect that quiets our restless mind so that we can begin to hear that inner symphony of the spirit.

The important thing to remember is that Logos meditation like all meditation techniques, is *only* a ship to bring you closer to God. The boat ride must never become more important than your destination. The boat is a *very useful vessel* for exploring new waterways within, but when you have sighted land in the Being of Christ, you will gladly leave your vehicle behind to walk the shores of that holy land.

Now we're ready to talk about what you may expect to experience as you meditate.

What is the experience of meditation?

A thousand words or thoughts about meditation could never substitute for the experience itself. Our human minds are limited by time and space, but to experience Christ-consciousness is to go *beyond* time and space. Our minds just don't have any pigeon-holes for such things. That's why the experience cannot be captured in words.

We can say, for instance, that meditation is *experiencing God*, which it is, but what does experiencing God *mean?* Though words always fall short, still we may be able to get an echo of what this experience is by listening to some of those who have been there. There are thousands of accounts, each different from the others and yet all strikingly similar. Thomas Merton wrote:

Our souls rise up from our earth like

Jacob waking from his dream and exclaiming: "Truly God is in this place and I knew it not!" God himself becomes the only reality in Whom all other reality takes its proper place—and falls into insignificance . . . A door opens in the center of our being and we seem to fall through it into immense depths which, although they are infinite, are all accessible to us; all eternity seems to have become ours in this one placid and breathless contact.

The highest states of meditation also seem to bring an overwhelming awareness of the unity of all things.

What we remember with joy from such experiences is that sense of *unity*, the feeling that we are a part of all that lives. The very stones and hills seem vividly alive; we find a meaning in everything— the seed in the ground, the bark on the tree, the sound of the cricket. We feel that there is something out there which is identical with something in ourselves (Ardis Whitman).

Johnston asserts that "Any Christian who sincerely meditates is becoming one with the universal Christ in a process that reaches its climax in resurrection, the ultimate universalization of man."

I think the experience is very much like being in love, only in this case your beloved is in all ways perfect, never leaves you nor forsakes you, has no faults, is changeless, eternal, infinite, and loves you unconditionally. St. John of the Cross spoke of his love affair with God metaphorically: "My beloved is the mountains, the solitary wooded valleys, strange islands . . . silent music."

Only by the grace of God . . .

Of course, we cannot expect instant Christ-consciousness as soon as we start to meditate. Nor can we *make* it happen. Such illuminating experiences of the presence of God come to us *only by the grace of God.* "We love, because he first loved us" (1 John 4:19). There is no magic formula that will take us to God by our own efforts. It is only through His grace that we come into His presence. The decision to meditate does not *begin* with us. It comes about in answer to the divine call. The fact that you are reading this book attests to the fact that you have heard that call at some time in your life. But just because illumination comes to us by grace does not mean that we can sit back and say, "OK, God, you do it for me." We must answer the call by opening our consciousness, by practicing the presence of God, and one of the very best ways of doing this is through meditation. It can help us to open our spiritual ears so that we may begin to hear the divine symphony. Though the music *may* break forth in a sudden *sforzando*, it is more likely to tiptoe in on muted tones. Michael Eastcott says it beautifully:

> The path of meditation can well be compared with the long stillness before daybreak. There is frequently nothing to mark it but a quietly increasing light. The gradual dawning of a new world in our consciousness comes silently. It is a secret, inner thing which we can never fully share with others—a silent path.

Meditation, then, is not just something we *do* twice a day; it is a way of life, a gradual *becoming* that increases the dimensions of our spirit.

How to use this book

In addition to its primary purpose, which is to experience God, regular meditation brings some other incidental gifts with it in the forms of: increased relaxation; decreased stress and anxiety; improved human relationships; greater harmony in the physical body; better control of emotions; heightened creativity; feelings of well-being; and a more integrated personality. It should also be a stimulus toward service to your fellow human beings. I'll be giving you specific meditations for each of these areas of your life, but always remember that the supreme goal of all Christian meditation is to be present to the Lord in love. *Please read Chapters 2 and 3 before you try any of the meditations in later chapters because the general principles involved in the meditation techniques are covered in those two chapters.*

Whatever you do, don't try to read through the whole book in a few sittings. That would be like trying to pour several gallons of orange juice into an eight-ounce glass. Most of it would be lost. Better to pour a glassful at a time, sipping it slowly and going back to the pitcher only when the previous glassful is fully digested.

Be gentle. Don't try to force anything. You can't make a flower bloom by pulling on it. All the best gardener can do is to keep the weeds out, expose the plant to the sun, and water and fertilize it regularly. This regularity, a sign of caring, is of greatest importance in meditation, also. Once or twice a week won't be enough to open your spiritual petals. If you're going to meditate at all, make up your mind to do it twice a day if at all possible and never less than once a day.

But what if you don't have time? Well, then it becomes a question of priorities. Every person has exactly the same number of hours and minutes every day. And at some level of mind, each decides how he's going to invest those hours. I'd suggest that you make a list of all the daily demands on your time. Then imagine you are ninety years old and looking back on your life. From *that* perspective, which things are the most important? Which ones have *lasting* value? Now number them in order of importance. If spiritual growth is so low on your list that you can't quite work it in, then there's no point in wasting your time with this book. But I have an idea that you and I were drawn together in the pages of this book because spiritual growth is *very* important to both of us. So—weed your garden.

When I first started meditating, all six members of our family were living at home, I was a part-time college teacher, a correspondent for a national newspaper, a Sunday school teacher, and a free-lance writer. How in the world could I ever find time to meditate twice a day? Well, I discovered an astonishing thing. The more regularly I meditated, the more I got done! Instead of *crowding* my day, it seemed to *ease* the congestion! It's because meditation drains off stress and helps us to *order* our lives. "He that is within me performs that which is appointed unto me" (Job 23:14). It's true!

One more thing I need to tell you before

we start: you will not be able to meditate with the same success every time. Don't be constantly evaluating your meditation. Don't worry about whether or not it's working. There will be times when you'll be soaring and other times when you can't seem to get off the ground. No matter. Let it come and go as it will. It's in God's hands, after all. There's no need to cling. Just continue on with your meditation, *keep on being regular*, and you'll soon pass through the desert places. As a matter of fact, I have found that those dry spells always seem to precede the periods of greatest growth. Tree leaves turn brown in the fall to give the tree a rest that will prepare it for the surge of growth that is to come in spring. So remind yourself, whenever your meditation feels barren, that *especially now* invisible forces are at work within you, preparing you for the next stage of new growth. Just don't stop watering!

There is no meditation technique that is appropriate for everyone. Try those that appeal to you (be sure to give them at least a three-week trial), and you'll soon know which ones feel right for you.

If you disagree with any of the ideas in

the book or find something that seems incompatible with your beliefs, just let it pass on by. No need to become upset. I don't expect you to agree with all I write here. You have to choose what is right for *you*. Reading a book is a little like shopping for clothes—you take what fits and leave the rest. I only hope that you will approach the book with a fresh mind, open to new possibilities. It would be a sad thing if Christians were to be unduly fearful or defensive about meditation. After all, God commanded it and, as long as we keep the communication lines open, *He will direct our journey*. When the way is right, you will know it. It will hit under your heart like a bird.

Oh Word made flesh, breathe in me.
Amen.

2

"Seek ye first the Kingdom of God"

A FEW months ago, the remote control that opens our electric garage door was on the blink. As we drove into our driveway one evening, my husband stopped the car and asked our eight-year-old son, John, to push the button inside the garage so we could drive in. As the door started to go up, I heard John's piercing screams. Leaping out of the car, I saw that the wind had slammed the heavy walk-through door on his finger and he was jumping up and down in pain. By the time I reached him and got the door open, his little finger on his left hand was bent and mangled.

I picked him up, ran back to the car, and we rushed to the emergency room of the hospital. The nurse laid him on an examining table and looked inside the tissues I'd wrapped around his finger.

"I'll get a doctor right away," she said,

and as she walked past me, she whispered, "He's going to lose it!"

It was grayish white and flat and though the skin was torn open, there was no blood. The circulation had been completely cut off. I realized, with a sense of horror, that the nurse was right. When she called our family physician and described John's injury, he told her to send for the orthopedic surgeon.

While we waited for both doctors to arrive, I said a short prayer. Then, holding on to John's right hand, I began to fill myself with Christ-consciousness. A feeling of warmth and light radiated through me, and I held onto this awareness of Christ's presence until our doctor arrived, about twenty minutes later.

The doctor removed the gauze the nurse had wrapped around John's finger and the nurse gasped. The bone was obviously broken, but the finger was no longer flat. The flesh was full and pink and natural looking, and the cut was bleeding. The circulation had started again!

As the doctor sewed up the cut and splinted the finger, the nurse kept shaking her head and saying, over and over, "I just don't understand it."

Well, I don't understand it, either. It's possible that it had nothing to do with my meditation. I only know that whenever I've had a need, if I've been able to first establish myself firmly in Christ-consciousness, the need has been met. The episode with John's finger is only one of many, many similar instances that have happened to me since I've been meditating. Don't misunderstand. I don't believe there is any magical power in meditation itself. It's just a tuning device, a way of invoking *God's* power. To me, it proves the validity of Christ's promise: "Seek ye first the kingdom of God and all these things shall be added unto you" (Luke 12:31).

But where is that kingdom, and how do we go about seeking it? Christ gave us the answer to both questions. In Luke 17:21 He said, "The kingdom of God is within you."

I had read those words so many times and heard them spoken from the pulpit again and again, but they had never really *meant* much to me until I started to meditate. I had no idea that it was actually possible to *experience* the kingdom of heaven right here in this earthly life. I had never been conscious of that kingdom within because I had been too busy frantically scurrying from one external goal to another, never finding true fulfillment. When I prayed, I would direct my attention outward, as if I were sending long-distance messages to a remote Being way off up in the sky somewhere, when all of the time, He was—and *is*—"closer than breathing, nearer than hands and feet" (Tennyson).

How to find the kingdom within

Then how can we become aware of that inner kingdom? *How* do we seek it? Again, we turn to Christ for our answer. We know that, throughout His earthly life, Jesus withdrew periodically from the multitudes and even from his disciples, going off by Himself to meditate. This is our supreme example. This is our key for seeking heaven while we are still on earth. We, too, need time by ourselves. We need to withdraw our attention, temporarily, from external distractions and learn to focus it ever more deeply inward, until we stand, literally, in the presence of God.

"Seek ye first the kingdom of God and all these things shall be added unto you." When we fully comprehend their meaning, we realize that these are among the most powerful words Jesus spoke. Still, it's possible to trip on them. If we seek the kingdom with our eyes fastened on "all these things" we want "added unto" us, we are sure to stumble and lose both the key to the kingdom and its reward. Though meditation can bring a rainbow of other blessings into our lives, its highest and most rewarding purpose is *to develop a deeper awareness of the presence of God within.*

If you have a problem or a need, by all means pray about it. Do everything you can to bring about the desired result. BUT (and I'm convinced this is often what makes the difference between answered and unanswered prayer), at some point (why not now?) you must LEAVE OFF seeking an answer to your prayer and seek, instead, the kingdom of God within. Nothing else will bring you lasting fulfillment; nothing less will satisfy the deep inner hunger that is, in truth, your soul's inborn homesickness for its Father. When you find your way "home," all these things *will* be added.

As I was thinking about this, a story formed in my mind that may help you to a clearer understanding of the absolute necessity of seeking first the kingdom of God.

A young man, a peasant in a faraway kingdom, was very dissatisfied with his life. There were so many things he wanted. He yearned for love, but he had grown up never knowing who his parents were, and no one seemed to care about him. He was hungry much of the time and so he begged for food and never had enough. Wearing rags, he dreamed of having elegant clothes. He longed for beauty but was surrounded by filth and ugliness.

This young man had heard that the king was loving and compassionate and often helped people in need, so he sent a message to the king, pleading for all the things he lacked. There was no answer, so he decided to go to the palace in person, in hopes that the king would grant his wishes.

He traveled for many days, and when he arrived he found the palace surrounded by a tall iron fence with sharp, spear-like posts. Fearing that the guard wouldn't open the gate for him, he climbed over it, tearing his clothes even more and gashing a wound in his chest.

Once inside the palace grounds, he saw a beautiful, golden-haired maiden strolling through the garden, and he was overcome by an unexplainable feeling of love. He decided to follow her, turning away from the direction of the palace. He could always go to the king later. But as he walked toward the maiden and she saw his shabby clothing, his matted hair, and his bleeding chest, she turned and ran away.

Sad but still determined to get the things he came for, the young man walked along through the perfectly kept gardens, marveling at the rows and rows of brightly colored flowers. Never in his life had he seen such beauty! He could see the palace in the distance, but right now, more than anything in the world, he wanted to hold the beauty of a rose in his hand. He reached down to pick one, but thorns—long, sharp ones—stabbed his hands till they bled.

He stumbled on, weak from hunger and aching with pain, until he came to a small orchard. He was half starved, and here was fruit—apples, peaches, pears, apricots—all he could eat! He decided to stop and eat before going on to the palace. It wouldn't take long. But all the fruit on the lower branches had been picked, so he climbed as high as he could in the huge apple tree and was just reaching for a piece of fruit when the branch he was standing on broke, and he fell to the ground, painfully wrenching his back.

He lay on the ground for a long time, cursing the world and hating himself. Maybe there *wasn't* a kind and loving king after all. Maybe those who had told him about the king were deluded or crazy or lying. Everything he thought he had wanted was here within these grounds, and yet he was more miserable than ever.

Still, he had come this far, and the

palace (if it wasn't a mirage) was just ahead of him, so he pulled himself up and hobbled on, finally crawling up the steps on his hands and knees. Too weak to knock, he cried out, "Please open the door. All I want is to see the king!"

No sooner had he said this than the huge door opened and he found himself inside, surrounded by a golden light, more glorious than anything he had ever seen. And he heard a gentle voice say, "My son! You've come home at last!"

The young man was bewildered and thoughts raced through his mind. He'd never known who his father was. Was this all a dream, or could it really be that he was a lost child of the king?

The voice spoke again. "Many years ago, when you were just a child, you wandered away from the palace. I've been searching for you ever since. I watched you climb over the fence without trying the gate. My son, the gate is never locked! I saw you pursuing love, grabbing at beauty, and straining after fruit that was beyond your grasp. Finally, when I saw you writhing on the ground in despair, I knew you had discovered what seeking men always discover sooner or later—that the kingdom without the king is never enough.

"Now that you have found your way home, all of the beauty, all of the fruit, all of my riches, all of the wisdom and love in the kingdom are yours. They always have belonged to you, but I couldn't give them to you until you found your way back to me. Welcome home, my son."

You and I don't need to experience the frustration of sending pleading messages to a far-away king because we know that *our* king is right here with us, no matter where we are. We don't need to scramble and grab to have what we need, as soon as we realize, in the deep inner center of ourselves, *who we are*.

There are many ways of coming into the presence of our Father. The first step is to realize that *He* has been searching for *us*, all of our lives, that the gate to the palace grounds is never locked, and that He is waiting within to welcome us home. Our most fervent prayer should always be, "I only want to see the King!"

Object meditation

One way of seeking the kingdom of God through meditation is to use an object as the focal point of your contemplation. Any of the Christian symbols, such as the cross, the fish, the dove, or a picture of Jesus can help you to develop a one-pointedness that will give you rich insights into your relationship with the living Christ. Claudio Naranjo, in the book, *On the Psychology of Meditation*, says of such objects: "Being symbols created by a higher state of consciousness, *they evoke their source* [italics added] and always lead the meditator beyond his ordinary state of mind, a beyondness that is the meditator's deepest self, and the presence of which is the very heart of meditation" (p. 15).

To do object meditation, sit in a comfortable chair and place the object in front of you at about eye-level. Keep enough distance between yourself and the object so that your eyes do not have to strain to focus easily on the symbol. Plan to meditate for a predetermined length of time. Since this is a very intense type of meditation, five minutes is about right at first. Later, you can increase the time. A kitchen timer, if you have one, will relieve you of the necessity of interrupting your meditation to check your watch or clock.

As you gaze at the symbol, try to become aware of the *essence* behind it. Through opening your consciousness to the symbol, you are placing yourself under the influence of the Being (Christ) that it represents. Do not stare at one spot but let your eyes move over the surface of the object, noticing its lines, colors, textures, reflections.

After you have examined it with your eyes for a while, you may want to pick it up. Run your fingers over its surface; turn it over in your hand; experience its essence through your sense of touch, *maintaining a constant awareness of what it represents*. If unrelated thoughts creep in (and they will!), simply notice them and gently return your attention to the object.

With repeated meditations, you will find the symbol taking on deeper and deeper meaning for you. It will become a vehicle for entering into the presence of God.

If you decide to do this type of meditation, stay with it every day for at least two or three weeks before going on to another form. We all have a tendency to expect instant results, but if we become impatient, we may find ourselves dashing from one technique to another and missing the whole thing.

When John was just a toddler, he became separated from me in a large department store. I went from department to department, asking the clerks if they'd seen a little boy in a green and yellow "Big Bird" shirt. Time and again, they answered, "He was here a few minutes ago, calling for his mommie, but he rushed away before we could help him find you." When we finally made connections, we agreed that if we ever became separated again, he'd stay right where he was and wait for me to find him. That's what we need to do in meditation. We need to stay in one place long enough for God to draw us to Him.

You may want to start with object meditation, or you may prefer to begin with a guided meditation. Following are two such meditations that may help you to find your way into that inner kingdom. All of the guided meditations in this book have come to me (or through me) in the space of inner stillness, when I have opened myself to God. The first one, "The Being of Light," came into my consciousness after I'd been meditating about a year, and I find myself returning to it again and again because it always makes me whole. It's the one I used the night John smashed his finger. The second, "The Ocean of Love," came to me after I had asked God for guidance in the writing of this book. After you have been meditating for a few months, you may want to develop some meditations of your own.

In using the guided meditations, it's best to choose one that seems to vibrate on your own frequency and then plan to use it every day for at least three weeks before going on to another. Set aside a time when you will not be disturbed for at least fifteen or twenty minutes. If you have a tape recorder, it may be helpful for you to record the meditation, so that you won't have to keep referring back to the book. Be sure to leave ample pauses at the appropriate places.

If you don't have a recorder, use the book this way: read until you come to a box (☐); then *close your eyes* and follow the directions given, visualizing each part of the meditation. Take your time. Don't go on until you truly *feel* and experience the scene being described. After a few times of doing this, you will be able to do the entire meditation without the book.

Sit in a comfortable chair that has a straight back. Don't try to meditate lying down. You might fall asleep. It is best not to wear any binding clothes, such as a tight belt or girdle that may interfere with your breathing or make you tense. You may want to remove your shoes.

Don't strain. Remember, the gate is always open. *He* seeks *you*. All you need to do is to be still and create a space for Him to come to you.

Guided meditation number one:
The Being of Light

Sit quietly for a short time, relaxing and letting go of any tension you may feel in your body.

Now close your eyes and direct your attention to a spot right in the center of your chest, at about the place where your ribs begin to separate. Inhale deeply, expanding your chest as far as you can. Now, hold that breath in as you say silently in your heart, "The kingdom of God is within me." Exhale, forcing as much of the air out of your lungs as you possible can. Repeat this five times. ☐

Now, with your attention still focused at the center of your chest, begin to visualize a tiny Being, about an inch high, standing on a soft white cloud, near your heart. Assume that this Being is Christ. He is clothed in a flowing white robe, and His hands are raised in blessing. There is a warm, compassionate smile on His face and His eyes glow with love. Look within now and see Him there. Feel His presence within you. ☐

Notice, now, that rays of gleaming light are radiating from the heart of this tiny Being. As you watch, His whole body becomes luminous, glistening. You begin to feel a pleasant warmth glowing within your heart where He stands. Experience that warmth and light. ☐

Now, slowly let this Being of light, the Christ within you, begin to grow. Let His warmth and light spread from that small spot, downward into your abdomen and upward into your lungs and heart, until His body fills your whole torso. Then feel Him growing again, until His head fills your head, His arms fill your arms, and His legs fill your legs. ☐

He now fills you completely and your whole body is bathed in holy light, both inside and out. It is a glistening, airy light that makes you feel almost weightless, an all-pervading light that gently consumes any impurities within your body and within your soul. Be still now and feel it. Let it happen. *Be* that light-filled, Christ-filled soul. ☐

Then gradually feel this Being of light diminishing in size again, until He is once again a tiny figure standing on a cloud in the center of your chest near your heart. ☐

Know, in the depths of your being, that He is always there. No matter where you are, no matter what events are happening in your outer world, He stands within your heart, loving you, guiding you, blessing you. ☐

Say a short prayer of thanksgiving, open your eyes, stretch if you feel like it, and return to your daily routine. During the day, if problems come up or if unpleasant emotions arise, return your thoughts momentarily to that tiny Being you carry within you; "see" the Christ light near your heart; *know* that He loves you.

Meditation number two:
The Ocean of Love

After you have been sitting quietly for a few minutes, relax by taking several deep breaths. Then close your eyes and envision yourself walking along a sandy beach on the shore of a tropical island. The air is balmy, tall palm trees are swaying softly behind you, and the sand is warm between your toes. The sun sprinkles diamonds over the surface of the water. The sea is calm, and its gentle waves lap rhythmically up on the shore, whispering, whispering, whispering, echoes of the great mysteries of the universe. Sit down in the sand and see it all; feel it all; hear it all— now. ☐

After you have been sitting there for a while, you become aware that this is not an ordinary ocean. This ocean is Love— infinite, boundless, eternal Love. It is the Love by which all things were created, the Substance from which all life emerged. This Ocean is the Love of God. A deep inner yearning arises in you—a longing for the unconditional, changeless, eternal Love that only this Ocean can give. Feel that yearning. Let it build up in you until it hurts. Feel the Ocean drawing you to it. ☐

Now see yourself getting up from where you've been sitting on the sand and walking toward the beckoning sea. As you wade into the warm water, you feel no fear. Like a sleepy child snuggling into its mother's lap, you relax into the buoyant, sustaining water. Let go now, and surrender yourself into that Ocean of Love. ☐

Let go some more. You are safe, secure, protected, loved. Let yourself be rocked by the rhythmic, swelling tides of the everlasting arms. ☐

Now imagine that your body is made of salt. Those absolutely pure, all-embracing waters begin to soak into you. As your porous body absorbs them, you feel, deep within your chest, a gentle stroking, stroking, stroking. It begins just below your ribs and flows up over your heart, your lungs, your throat. Feel those cleansing waters now, stroking away all of the pain, hurt feelings, rejection, loneliness, loss, and grief you've been unable to let go of. ☐

As the love of God continues to wash over

you, in waves . . . and waves . . . and waves, feel your body of salt dissolving, melting, merging into that Ocean of Love, until there is only One, and you are part of that One. ☐

At this moment, *you are love*. No longer is there any pain of loneliness, any sense of separation, any feeling of grief or loss. There is only love. Feel it, Know it. *Be* it. ☐

Now slowly let the rolling tide flow back to the shore. Feel the salt crystals reforming about your being—arms, legs, torso, head. The salt becomes flesh again. Only now you are something more than flesh. Deep in the center of your being, beyond body, beyond thought, beyond emotion, there is a treasure chest from the sea, a gift to you from the infinite Ocean of Love. You carry within you the unspeakable mystery of divine Love. ☐

Open your eyes now, and give thanks.

Blessed God of Love, thank you for swaddling me in Your loving arms, for helping me to know that there is a harbor within me where the living waters ever roll, in waves of eternal Love. Amen.

3

Relaxation through meditation

MY father was a doctor—an old-fashioned, twenty-four-hour-a-day doctor who made house calls to farm homes in snowstorms in the middle of the night. He was usually up at 7:00 for surgery, and his office hours lasted till there were no more patients waiting, which was often 7:00 or 8:00 at night. But he always came home at noon, and before eating, he went in the den and closed the door for a half hour of quiet time alone. He called this his "daily dose of silence," and I know now that it was this time of stillness and quiet renewal that gave him the strength to endure the long hours and that kept alive the positive outlook that was so much a part of his character.

In our modern, pressure-cooker world, where the most frequently prescribed drugs are tranquilizers, the need for my father's prescription for daily doses of silence is greater than ever.

I used to ask my dad what he did during his quiet time and his answer was always the same. "I just sit still and clear my mind —get in tune with the Infinite. It relaxes me and brings me peace. I can't really say *how* I do this. Everyone has to find his own way."

It wasn't until many years later that I began, in earnest, to search for "my own way." I have always been a devout Christian, and prayer and meditation have been an integral part of my life. But the meditation I did was random and wandering and it didn't bring me the relaxation and peace my father had found.

Then I began studying the subject of meditation and learned about a technique called centering prayer, which involves the repetition of a sacred word. I first became acquainted with this form of contemplation while reading the works of Thomas Merton. Then, as I began studying the writings of other great Christian mystics, I discovered that devout Christians throughout the centuries have used repetitive prayer as a means of quieting the mind and getting "in tune with the Infinite." For the past five years, I have used a similar type of meditation as part of my Christian prayer life, and it has brought me not only deep relaxation but also a serenity and peace beyond words.

Before I give you step-by-step instructions for practicing this technique, I think it is important for you to realize that meditation is not an unconscious state. Instead of loss of consciousness, you will experience *heightened* awareness, increased perception, alert restfulness. I also want to assure you that the good things that will happen to you as a result of meditation have nothing to do with any "magical powers." The only power involved is *God's* power, and meditation is a lens that *focuses* that power.

In the past ten years or so, there has been a proliferation of popular offerings in meditation techniques (such as Transcendental Meditation and Dr. Herbert Benson's *The Relaxation Response*, among others), which are taught without any religious connotations. These can be very helpful for relaxation and stress release, but unless they are used for the purpose of coming closer to God, they are still the kingdom without the king. True and *lasting* peace can be found only through communion with God.

Logos meditation: what is it?

To avoid confusion with other systems, I have chosen the term Logos meditation. I think the Greek word *Logos*, which was translated as "the Word" in the first chapter of John, better describes what the technique means to Christians. In Logos meditation, we recognize the living Word and focus our attention on the Christ within. By opening your heart to God through Christ-centered meditation, you can clear out the mental and emotional debris that has been clogging up the spiritual conduit that connects you with God. Then His blessings can flow through freely, enriching your life in undreamed-of ways.

Let's take a minute to look at the first chapter of John.

In the beginning was the Word, and the

Word was with God, and the Word was God. The same was in the beginning with God. All things were made by him, and without him was not anything made that was made. In him was life, and the life was the light of men. And the light shineth in darkness, and the darkness comprehended it not (John 1:1–5).

The Word, of course, refers to Christ. It is the Word that speaks through man when he has become aware of the Christ within himself. When we grasp the significance of the statement, "All things were made by him" (the Word—Christ), we realize that, in using Christ's words as the focus of our meditation, we are tuning in to the creative power of God! That's what Logos meditation is all about.

Setting the scene

Keeping that in mind, let's begin by setting the scene for your meditation. It's a good idea to meditate in the same place each day, whenever possible. This helps you to "settle in" more easily, by creating a mental set and an air of expectancy, so that when you enter the special room and sit in that same chair, your mind automatically begins to calm down and tune in. I meditate in our living room because it has doors I can close. That room has become a holy place for me. When I go in there, close the door, and sit down in "my" chair, there is a certain feeling of holiness that hovers in the very air. It surrounds me, wraps me in inner stillness. It's like coming home at night after a hard day's work. It's as if, between meditations, I've gone out into the external world where I live my life, enjoy my family and friends, and do my work. Then, at night, I come "home" again, into the spiritual kingdom, for refreshment and renewal.

So find your own private place to meditate. If you use a bedroom I'd advise against sitting on the bed, because that arouses the mental set you normally associate with sleep. So take a chair in with you if there isn't already one there. Some people like to meditate outdoors and if the weather is pleasant, this can be very refreshing. I have a friend who lives in an apartment with her husband and two small children. She had trouble finding a place where she could be alone, so she meditates in her parked car. You'll find your special place.

Of course, there will be times when you can't meditate in the usual place. Then make do with whatever place you have. This will become easier after you've been meditating regularly for a while. I recently meditated for sixty miles in the back seat of a car full of lively teen-agers, with the tape player blaring rock-and-roll music in my ear. It was one of the best meditations I've had. But without the solid ground of regular "home base" meditations behind me, I probably would have become hopelessly frustrated.

It's a good idea to set aside a regular time of the day for meditation, too. If you decide to wait until you have all your work done or happen to have some free time, that time may never come. If, instead, you schedule it into your day and make up your mind to let nothing short of an emergency interfere, it will soon become as natural a part of your day as your daily bath. If you don't think you have time to meditate, please reread the section about that in Chapter 1.

The time of day you choose will depend on several factors. Meditation is more effective before meals than after eating because of the metabolic activity that takes place in your body after eating. If you wake up alert and eager for the day to begin, you may like to meditate before breakfast and then again before the evening meal. Since I'm a "night person," I found, by trying it, that early morning was just not a very good time for me to meditate. Now I do it before lunch and again in the evening after I get John to bed. If possible, set aside fifteen to twenty minutes twice a day for meditation.

You may find that it helps you to set up a little "altar" using a picture of Jesus, a cross, a Bible, or maybe even a candle or incense to create a sacred atmosphere where you meditate, though it's not necessary. Your internal atmosphere is far more important than any externals.

Warm-up exercises

You'll be more relaxed when you sit down to meditate if you do a little bit of mild physical exercise first, to loosen up tight muscles. This is especially important if you've had a nerve-jangling day or you're feeling tense.

Here are some nonstrenuous "warm-ups" for you to try. Don't feel you have to go through this pre-meditation routine every time, though. You'll know when you need it.

1. While still standing, begin shaking your right hand, from the wrist down. Shake it as hard as you can for about fifteen seconds; then shake both your hand and forearm for another fifteen seconds or so, and finally, shake your whole arm from the shoulder down, keeping your hand and lower arm loose and floppy at the same time. Do this until it begins to get tiring, and then let your hand fall to your side. It will feel feather-light and completely relaxed. Repeat this with your left hand.

2. Then, bracing yourself with your hand on a table or against the wall, do the same thing with each foot and leg, progressing from the ankle joint to the knee joint to the hip joint.

3. Now roll your shoulders around in circles, five times forward and then five

times backward. Then massage those muscles that begin at the base of your neck and extend outward to your shoulders. Really dig in if they're very tight.

4. Let your head drop forward till your chin almost touches your chest; then begin to roll your head all the way around, three times clockwise and three times counter-clockwise.

5. Next, with your hands on your hips, bend at the waist and rotate your upper body in first one direction and then the other.

6. Now sit down (aaah!), and if you still feel body tension, try this. Tighten up the muscles in your feet and then let go, saying to yourself, "My feet are relaxed and heavy." Tense and relax in sequence, your lower leg, thigh, and hip muscles and say, "My lower legs, thighs, and hips are heavy, relaxed, and comfortable." Do the same thing with your hands, lower and upper arms. Now pull in on your abdominal muscles and let go; tense and then relax your chest (pectoral) muscles and say, "The whole central portion of my body feels heavy, quiet, and relaxed." Finally, scrunch up your shoulders and tense your

neck muscles as hard as you can and then relax, saying, "I feel all the tension in my neck letting go, letting go. It is relaxed." Finish with "My whole body feels quiet, comfortable, calm, and relaxed."

Deep breathing

You are now ready for some deep breathing. You should do this before meditating, even when you don't do the other exercises.

Slowly counting to seven, breathe in as much air as your lungs will take. Then hold the breath in for another seven seconds and slowly exhale, taking another seven seconds to empty your lungs as completely as you can. Repeat this five times.

Now your body should feel quite relaxed, but it will soon tense up again unless the inner you is calm and peaceful, too. That's where Logos meditation comes in.

Logos meditation: the procedure

So how do you do Logos meditation? The answer is, you don't *do* it. You let it happen to you. The Word (Christ) is already within you. In Romans 10:8, Paul said, "The word is nigh thee, even in thy mouth, in thy heart." The trouble is that our minds are so busy carrying on a constant internal monologue that we can't hear the Word within. To prove this to yourself, try to sit still for three minutes without having any thoughts, without letting any words come into your mind. I'm sure you'll find it impossible. Your mind is like a lake, in the depths of which lies the living Word, but you can't see past the surface because the water is so choppy. Thoughts jump and splash and dart in all directions like restless fish, muddying up the water and obscuring what lies below the surface. But if you consciously focus your attention on a *single* thought and keep repeating that one thought over and over, you begin to set up a sequence of steady, even waves, all coming from the same direction, that override the choppy water and smooth out the surface of the lake. Gradually, the waves become deeper, gentler, calmer, until you see beyond the surface and touch the living Presence within.

Does this mean that all other thoughts

will stop? No. You'll continue to have "fish" swimming in and out. I'll give some suggestions for dealing with those in a minute.

I'm now going to give you a Logos that has helped to change the quality of my life. The words are not mine. They are Jesus' and you already know them, but you will soon come to know them in a deeper, more personal way. He first spoke them to comfort His disciples, but He speaks them also for you and for me. The words are alive and active, here and now. The Logos is: "Peace I leave with you, my peace I give to you" (John 14:27).

1. Begin your meditation by sitting quietly with *closed eyes*, visualizing yourself surrounded by a softly glowing white light. Christ, who is infinite light, pure love, the living Word, is in the room with you now. He is as real at this moment as your faith will permit Him to be.

2. Listen within yourself until you can hear His words resonating there. "Peace I leave with you, my peace I give to you." Begin to pronounce the words aloud, as if you were speaking along with the inner

voice that is whispering them. Continue to repeat them aloud, over and over.

3. After a while, you will notice that the Logos seems to be moving. Your *mouth* is saying it, but it seems to be seated within you—in your head, your throat, your stomach, or your chest. When you feel it moving inward, let your lips fall silent and continue repeating the words internally. Eventually, you will feel them resonating in your heart. St. John of the Cross, who used the Jesus Prayer (Blessed Lord Jesus, have mercy on me), wrote, "After no great lapse of time I had the feeling that the Prayer had, so to speak, by its own action passed from my lips to my heart. Further, there came into my heart a gracious warmth."

4. Do not be concerned about the speed or rhythm in which you repeat the words. They will find their own natural rhythm, and this will change during your meditation, according to your state of consciousness. Do not attempt to coordinate the Logos with your breathing. It may or may not fall into a pattern that synchronizes with your breathing. It

doesn't matter. Just let it pass beyond your conscious control and it will flow naturally.

5. Don't be upset if you suddenly realize you've been thinking about something else and have forgotten all about your Logos. Whenever a stray thought comes into your mind, just calmly notice the thought; then let go of it and gently return your mind to your Logos. It's stress that causes the thoughts to intrude, so each time you let go of a thought and return to your Logos, you're releasing some of your accumulated inner pressure. As your mind calms down and centers in, you'll notice that thoughts are still going through, but they're not holding your attention. I can't say exactly how it will be with you, but maybe sharing with you part of my own inner experience with thoughts during meditation will give you some idea of what to expect. Here is a page from the "spiritual journal" I keep.

Wednesday. February 23, 1977. There seems to be a perfectly balanced, lightly suspended *space* in me where the Logos moves and changes. The changing images I was aware of during meditation today looked something like this:

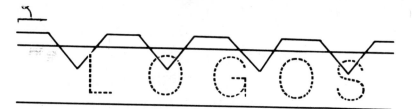

a. *First few minutes.* Thoughts were like teeth, biting into the Logos.

b. *Next time space.* Thoughts dipped in but didn't touch the Logos. Then they floated on by.

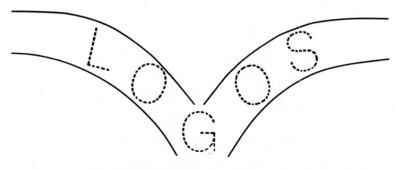

c. *After about fifteen minutes of meditation.* When I was deeply into meditation, the Logos seemed to be pouring itself downward or inward. Thoughts must have occurred, but I really didn't notice them at all.

Visualization may make it easier for you to let go of your uninvited thoughts. You may want to convert them mentally into birds and watch them fly away, or see them as bubbles rising within you and watch them float up to the surface of the water and disappear. I'll go into these visualization techniques further in Chapter 4.

6. Be gentle. Do not force or strain. Do not try to *concentrate* on the Logos. This form of meditation is definitely *not* concentration. It is the exact opposite. It is a letting go, a giving up of thoughts. At first, you will find yourself thinking of the meaning of the Logos words, and this is good. Later, they will just pass through you, going steadily about their business of clearing and calming your mind and soul. They are living, self-propelled Words. They are Logos—the Word—Christ in you. Christ does not need your concentration to perform His work, only your open heart.

7. Always close each meditation period with a prayer. Though meditation is, itself, a form of prayer, it should not take the place of other forms of worship. I think you'll find that it has the power to add marvelous depth and beauty to your prayer life. Your Bible

reading will begin to take on deeper significance, and your worship at church will become more and more meaningful when you have opened yourself, through meditation, to the living Presence within.

8. When your meditation time is finished, do not jump up right away and return to physical activity. Keep your eyes closed for a minute or so as you begin to stir around. You may feel like stretching. Then open your eyes and sit there another minute or so before getting up. Meditation slows down your breathing, heart rate, and other body functions, so you need a short transition period between such a relaxed state and your normal activity.

9. After you have been meditating for fifteen to twenty minutes twice a day for some time, let the Logos begin to expand out into your daily life. When you wake up in the morning, let the inner words remind you of Christ's presence within you. When you feel upset, tune in to your Logos, repeating it silently in your heart. As you are settling your mind for sleep, let all disturbing thoughts dissolve into the Logos. Your sleep will be peaceful and refreshing.

10. If you want to use an external aid to

help you keep the Logos in your awareness, you might try using prayer beads. I happen to belong to a Protestant denomination, but when I was a little girl, we had a Catholic girl who lived with us. We shared a room, and every night she would lie in bed silently saying her rosary before she fell asleep. I remember looking over at her from the other twin bed and noticing the blissful expression on her face. Whenever she was worried or anxious about anything, I always knew where I'd find her—in our room, sitting on her bed with her rosary in her hands. How I envied her! How I wished that I could have a rosary of my own! But Mother said those were only for Catholics and I wasn't a Catholic, so that was that.

Well, I found out that you don't have to be a Catholic to use prayer beads. Meditators from all faiths have used them. A few months ago, I bought some wooden beads in the five-and-ten-cent store, strung them, and tried meditating with them. They do help keep your attention focused on the inner words, as you pass the beads through your fingers with each repetition of the Logos. Sometimes I use them when I meditate; sometimes I don't. When I use them, this is what happens (from my journal):

Tuesday, April 5, 1977. I like meditating with my beads. The first time around the circle, it's like knitting. I'm *doing* something. It works off tension. The second time around, *it* does *me*. It's much slower then, less deliberate; the Logos sings in me. After two times around, my hands stop. The Logos isn't singing now; it just hangs there in my heart-space. It is no longer words; it is Spirit breathing on me.

Well, the main thing to keep in mind if you decide to use beads, or any other external aid, is that *they are only tools*—nothing more. The same is true of the Logos meditation technique or any other meditation method. They are forms of prayer, ways of opening the heart so that, *by the grace of God*, we may receive the Holy Spirit. They must never become ends in themselves.

Of course, the Logos I have given you here is not the only one you may use, although it has been special for me, and I think it's a very good one to begin with.

Later, I'd suggest going off by yourself and quietly asking God to give you a Logos that is just right for you. The word or words should be deeply expressive of your love for Him. Not just any words will do. I think it's important to choose words that originated in the Spirit, words that are truly inspired, because a Logos invokes the higher state of consciousness from which it was conceived.

Music meditation

I can't close this chapter dealing with relaxation without inviting you to fly with me on the wings of music meditation. You don't have to be a musician; you don't even have to *know* anything *about* music to borrow its wings. All you need is a record player and some inspirational music. If you don't have this, you may be able to find some fitting music on the radio. Hymns, especially instrumental arrangements without vocalists, are excellent. Classical music is fine, too, particularly the uplifting strains of such composers as Bach and Beethoven. Try to arrange it so the music will play continuously for at least fifteen to thirty minutes.

Background music is one thing; group singing of Christian songs is another thing; but music meditation is neither of these and at its best, it can be better than either. Sometimes at night, after I get John to bed, and if no one else is needing my attention, I go in the living room, close the door, turn the record player on and the lights off, lie down on the couch, and do music meditation in the dark. It is much more than just listening, though. It's a merging of self with that which is beyond self.

To come into the presence of Christ on the wings of music, it is best to be alone. Do not try to knit or read or do anything else while you listen. Close your eyes or, if it's night-time, turn off the lights, so that you will not be distracted by visual stimuli. Lie down in a comfortable position. Then give your full attention to the music. Listen with your heart, not your ears.

Imagine that the music flows into the room on a beam of silver-white light, from a heavenly source. Let that beam of light dip directly down into your heart and pass through it, rising up again into the clouds. As the music continues to swell, let yourself be pulled upward by it, heart-first, as if you were soaring through the air on silver-white wings. Just climb onto the music and ride with it,

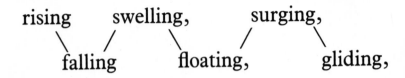

until you *become* the music.

I can't tell you *how* to do this, and nothing at all may happen the first few times you try it. Then one night, when your heart is open, you will begin to feel the invisible pull. Go with it. Stay with it. Let God be with you.

Let the silver-white ray of music transport you beyond yourself into the farthest reaches of the universe. Let the sound of the music expand and grow, until it bounces off the clouds of time and echoes against the edges of infinity. Let yourself merge into the timeless, spaceless, eternal presence of God.

When the last chords of music fade away and the silver-white wings fold back into your heart, you will find yourself in the presence of a silence more profound than any you have ever known before. In the still hush of this moment, offer your soaring heart into the eternal stillness. With a prayer in your heart, give your winged soul to God.

Loving Creator of all that is, whose Substance fills the universe, I know that I can never drift beyond the wings of Your love. You are my beam of light that shines in the darkness; let me be a singing note in Your eternal Song. Amen. Amen.

4

Meditation as worry therapy

> Worry is a form of atheism.
> —*Fulton Sheen*

IF you had an infection in your body, you surely would not take arsenic to heal yourself. Yet most of us do the mental equivalent of that every time a problem arises in our lives. We drink in spiritual poison, and the name of this poison is worry.

We all know that it isn't what *happens* to us in our lives that makes us happy people or unhappy people. It's how we *react* to what happens. Meditation can help us to *choose* how we're going to react. Shakespeare said, "There is nothing either good or bad but thinking makes it so." Though we can't always change the *events* of our lives, we can, in the quiet chamber of our hearts, transform our attitudes from worry and despair to hope and faith. Just as our body's heart can deliver medicine to an aching back or a throbbing head, our soul's heart can, in the silence of meditation, smooth a healing balm on troubled feelings and heal the canker sores of worry.

One of my friends was recently taken to the hospital with a severe attack of colitis. When I went to visit her, she told me, "The doctor says that worry is literally eating me up inside and I know he's right, but I just can't help it. When you know your teenage daughter is on drugs and staying out all night with boys, you can't help worrying. I *know* worrying doesn't do any good, but just knowing that doesn't help me to stop *doing* it."

My friend was right. We need something more than just the realization that worry is a destructive poison. We need an antidote, something to neutralize the poison and wash it out of our systems. Meditation can be that healer.

Why are you *choosing* to worry?

I'm going to give you some specific meditation techniques for overcoming worry, but first, let's see if you have any unconscious reasons for hanging onto your worry habits.

St. Paul wrote, "God has not given us the Spirit of fear but of power and of love and of a sound mind" (2 Timothy 1:7). Can that be true? If God really did give us the spirit of a sound mind, why aren't we manifesting it? Ask yourself these questions:

Am I sure I *want* to be free from worry? If you think this is a ridiculous question, ask further:

Is worry bringing me any rewards, such as sympathy from others or justification for self-pity?

Does worry give me an excuse for going to bed, taking pills, having a cocktail?

Does it relieve me of the feeling of responsibility for solving my problems?

Do I feel I really *should* be worrying? This is a tricky one. You may feel, somewhere inside you, that worry is a sign of caring. If the people around you are worrying, you may feel guilty if you don't join in. *Caring* about your problems and those of others brings constructive action, but *worrying* about them actually paralyzes your problem-solving ability. We learn the worry habit. How many times have you heard someone say something like this to a child: "How can you be so cheerful when Grandma is so sick?" Would it do Grandma any good to have the child creeping around with a pained look on his face? Of course not! So think about it. Are you shaming yourself into worry?

Consider thoughtfully the above questions, and if you recognize any of these subtle strings pulling you into the worry trap, make up your mind to break those strings. You've already taken the first step if you've recognized that there *are* some unconscious reasons for your worry habit. Then ask yourself if you're willing to give up the subtle rewards of worry for the infinitely greater treasure of peace of mind. If your answer is yes, earmark your next three meditation periods for string-cutting.

Guided meditation number 3: string-cutting

Note: This meditation does not deal with the worries themsleves but with your unconscious motivations for clinging to worry patterns. Follow the directions given in Chapter 2 for using the guided meditations. Either tape-record them or else pause at the boxes, close your eyes, and visualize each part before going on to the next.

1. Go to your quiet place, get comfortable, and relax as completely as you can. (See exercises in Chapter 3.) ☐

2. Now visualize yourself standing at the bottom of a dark basement. Look up and see the stairs rising through an opening in the ceiling. At the top of the stairs you can see sunshine, blue sky, and soft white clouds. Picture this now. ☐

3. Do you want to go from the darkness into the light? Then start climbing. As you take the first step, think of one of the worry rewards that's holding you back (such as sympathy from others, or whatever you discovered when you answered the above questions). ☐

4. Name it. *Feel* it as a tight string around

your ankle, binding you to the darkness. ☐

5. Next, notice that, on the step above you, there's a pocket knife. Pick it up, reach back in your mind, and cut that string. Do it with gusto. Really *snap* that binder and experience the relief and sense of freedom this brings. ☐

6. Then take another step, naming a different worry motivation, and cut another string, continuing to do this until you are rid of them all. ☐

7. Now *walk through* that bright opening and claim that spirit of "power and of love and of a sound mind" that is your birthright as a child of God. ☐

8. Sit there for a few more minutes, feeling the shimmering white light of Christ's peace surrounding you. ☐

Repeat this during the next two meditation periods, and go back to it any time you feel those subtle strings pulling you back into the worry habit.

Now you're ready to begin working on the worries themselves. Read through the following meditation techniques for dealing with worry and choose one that seems appropriate for your situation at this time. At another time, one of the others may be more fitting.

Problem-solving through meditation

This meditation is based on the principle that the best way to cope with worry is to take some kind of positive action. If you're worried about something you said to someone last night, you may want to call the person and apologize or explain what you meant. If you're concerned about a speaking engagement you have next week, you can begin writing your speech. But what if you don't *know* what action to take? Then take your problem to God in meditation.

1. Begin with a prayer of relinquishment, admitting to Him that you cannot solve this problem by yourself and that you're giving it to Him.

2. It may help to write out what the

problem is, listing possible solutions and the advantages and disadvantages of each.

3. Then go to your meditation place and prepare yourself for Logos meditation. (You may want to reread the section in Chapter 3 on this procedure.) Use the Logos, "He perfects that which concerns me" (Psalm 138:8). Or you may prefer to make the wording more immediate: "At this very moment, God is bringing the perfect answer to the problem that concerns me." Begin to repeat this to yourself, letting the meaning of the words penetrate your consciousness.

4. Your thoughts will probably soon be drawn back to the problem. When this happens, just calmly return to the Logos. As you begin to relax and center in on the infinite, let the Logos change to the single word, *perfection*.

5. When the worry creeps back in, mentally lay the word *perfection* over the problem, letting the Logos soak up the worry thought the way a sponge absorbs spilled coffee.

6. Continue doing this for about fifteen minutes. Then let the Logos go, leaving your mind clear and open, waiting,

listening. Don't try to force an answer. Just be an open channel for the divine message. The answer may come as a sudden flash of insight, a deep inner knowing. This may not happen during your meditation period. It may rise up through your unconscious mind later in the day when you're washing the dishes or driving to work or doing some other mundane task. It may leap from the page of a book you're reading or flash into your mind in a dream or during that half-way state between waking and sleeping early in the morning or as you're falling asleep. Some of my best ideas have jolted me awake in the middle of the night after I've been meditating about a particular problem for several days.

What this meditation does is to unclog your inner mind so that God can get His perfect answer through to you. I'm sure you've experienced the frustration of trying to call someone on the phone and repeatedly getting the busy signal. When your mind is constantly busy with worried thoughts, God gets the busy signal, no matter how fervently you've prayed for an answer to your problem. But when you still those thoughts through meditation, you free the line for God's call.

When you feel you have the answer, simply go ahead and do what needs to be done. It will be done with effectiveness and perfection because the action will flow through you from its transcendent Source. "He that is within me perfects that which concerns me."

But there's always the question, "How will I know that my answer is really from God?" Well, sometimes it will be very clear and you'll have no doubt. At other times, you may not be so sure. The best thing to do, if you're sure your action won't interfere with someone else's good, is to go ahead and proceed with it. The Bible says, "All things work together for good to them that love the Lord" (Romans 8:28). Dedicate the action to God, blessing it and commanding it to bring forth its good. At the same time, continue to meditate daily using the Logos, "He perfects that which concerns me." Keep the lines open, and He will make you aware of any changes of direction that need to be made.

Here is a poem by Lowell Fillmore that

says something very profound about problem-solving through meditation.

The Answer

When for a purpose
I had prayed and prayed and prayed
Until my words seemed worn and bare
    With arduous use,
And I knocked and asked and
    knocked and asked again,
And all my fervor and persistence
    brought no hope,
I paused to give my weary brain a rest
And ceased my anxious human cry.
    In that still moment,
After self had tried and failed,
There came a glorious vision of God's
    power.
And lo, my prayer was answered in
    that hour.

Walking meditation

Another way to defeat worry is through a walking meditation. This form of meditation combines physical exercise, fresh air, and inspired words. It's one of the best prescriptions I know for relieving anxiety and tension and dispelling worry. It doesn't matter what time of day you do it, but plan it into your daily schedule whenever you're feeling worried or tense. The few minutes you invest in it will be more than repaid with dividends of increased energy and feelings of well-being. One lady in my Sunday School class on meditation put it this way: "It's like spending a dollar and getting back a hundred dollars."

1. Choose a Bible quotation or a one-sentence prayer that really speaks to your situation. You may want to use one of the examples below or find one of your own choosing.

2. Then, put on your coat, tell the family you'll be back in a few minutes, and take a walk with God! Go alone or, if you go with someone else, agree not to talk. Repeat the passage over and over as you walk, letting the words flow naturally through your consciousness. The words may or may not fall into a rhythm with your footsteps. It doesn't matter.

3. Continue your walk for at least ten minutes. (You may enjoy it enough to want

to make it longer!) Here are some one-liners to use *if* . . .

a. *You have a tough decision to make:* "Thou shalt guide me with Thy counsel" (Psalm 73:24).

b. *You are feeling guilty:* "Renew a right spirit within me" (Psalm 51:10).

c. *You're tense but don't know why:* "Peace I leave with you, my peace I give unto you" (John 14:27).

d. *You're overly tired:* "I wait on the Lord to renew my strength; I shall run, and not be weary; I shall walk, and not faint" (Isaiah 40:31).

e. *Someone has wronged you:* "If God be for me, who can be against me?" (Romans 8:31).

f. *You're feeling fearful or worried:* "God has not given me the spirit of fear; but of power, and of love, and of a sound mind" (2 Timothy 1:7).

g. *You are unsure of yourself:* "I can do all things through Christ which strengtheneth me" (Philippians 4:13).

h. *You have too much to do:* "I cast my burden on the Lord, and He sustains me" (Psalm 55:22).

i. *You are feeling lonely:* "He will never leave me, nor forsake me" (Hebrews 13:5).

j. *You have financial worries:* "My God shall supply all my need according to his riches in glory by Christ Jesus" (Philippians 4:19).

k. *You are grieving:* "He healeth the broken in heart, and bindeth up their wounds" (Psalm 147:3).

l. *You are afraid:* "The Lord is the strength of my life; of whom shall I be afraid?" (Psalm 27:1).

m. *You are nervous about something you have to do:* "Thou wilt keep me in perfect peace because my mind is stayed on thee" (Isaiah 26:3).

I have used all of these at various times and have received blessed reassurance from them. The afternoon before my daughter's school play she was suddenly seized by an attack of stage-fright. I thought of suggesting that she study her lines some more, but I changed my mind. We went for a silent walk instead, meditating on "Thou wilt keep me in perfect peace because my mind is stayed on thee." I substituted Karen's name for "me" and "her" for "my." We agreed not to talk, but we stopped to pet a dog, picked up a few unusually pretty stones on a graveled road, smelled some lilacs, and watched the sky turn from a bright glare to a soft, restful pumpkin color.

When we got home, Karen was relaxed. The stagefright was gone, the play went well, and she had discovered a very effective tranquilizer—one that can't be purchased in any pharmacy.

Walking meditation may not solve your problem for you, but it will give you the spiritual strength and energy to cope with it more effectively. Also, because it focuses your mind on God instead of on your worry, it is very likely to give you a whole new perspective on your problem.

The foregoing meditations will help you to cope with *specific* worries, but sometimes you may feel anxious or depressed without knowing why. You just have a general overall feeling of uneasiness that won't go away. When this happens, try the chalkboard meditation.

Chalkboard meditation

This meditation just gradually evolved for me at a time when I was having trouble with worry thoughts intruding on my meditation. In fact, the first thought-seeds for this book grew out of this meditation.

1. Prepare yourself for meditation by doing the physical exercises given in Chapter 3.

2. Then sit comfortably, relax, and center in.

3. Now close your eyes and draw a chalkboard in your mind's eye. Make it large enough to cover the whole area in front of you, but leave it blank.

4. Now print the word PEACE in the center of the board and begin repeating it as the Logos for your meditation.

5. Before long, a stray thought will float into your consciousness. Just *notice* it, pay attention to what area of your life it relates to, and then erase it.

6. Reprint the word PEACE on the chalkboard.

7. Continue to do this with each new thought that comes into your awareness,

being sure, each time, to note what the thought pertains to before letting it go.

8. You will soon notice that a pattern is beginning to emerge. Your mind will keep returning to the disturbing area or areas of your life. Often, you will find that your depression or anxiety is caused by something you didn't even realize was troubling you! It may help to write down the thoughts you remember when you finish your meditation. Once you have discovered the source of your mental anguish, you can work on it directly through the other meditations in this chapter.

I told you this book grew out of this kind of meditation. Maybe it will help you to see how it works if I describe my experience for you.

Several months ago, I seemed to have reached some kind of plateau in my spiritual quest. I was troubled by a vague feeling of uneasiness, even though I didn't have any specific worries. When I meditated, my thoughts were more distracting than usual. I decided to take a closer look at those disrupting thoughts, and when I sat down to meditate and closed my eyes, the chalkboard just "appeared." The idea of noticing my thoughts and then erasing them was a natural outgrowth of that. My meditation went something like this: (Though my thoughts weren't evenly spaced, I'll simplify it by recording just three PEACE repetitions between thoughts.)

" . . . PEACE . . . PEACE . . . PEACE . . . first thought—about the writing classes I teach . . . PEACE . . . PEACE . . . PEACE . . . second thought—about an article I had written for *Guideposts* magazine . . . PEACE . . . PEACE . . . PEACE . . . third thought—about a passage in a book I was reading on meditation . . . PEACE . . . PEACE . . . PEACE . . . fourth thought—about a problem one of my children was having . . . PEACE . . . PEACE . . . PEACE . . . fifth thought—about the book I'd written on hearing loss . . . PEACE . . . PEACE . . . PEACE . . . sixth thought —about my feelings of being at a spiritual standstill . . . PEACE . . . PEACE . . . PEACE . . . seventh thought—about a guided meditation I'd

written for my Sunday school class . . .
PEACE . . . PEACE . . . PEACE . . . "

I wrote down the above thoughts in my journal, and when I read them through, I realized that all but one of them pertained to writing or meditation. It wasn't a very big step from that point to the realization that my "stale" state of mind was due to the fact that I am happiest when I am writing or meditating, and that I had not written anything for quite a while. In that moment, I recognized the first faint stirrings of my desire to write a book on Christian meditation. As soon as I started working on the book, my undefined anxiety lifted, and my own meditations grew deeper and richer.

I return to the chalkboard meditation whenever I feel restless or uneasy or whenever I just feel vaguely dissatisfied or unfulfilled. It has never failed to dredge up the cause of my "dis-ease" and to leave the word PEACE written on the chalkboard of my soul.

Another meditation that helps with undefined worry feelings is the Divine Filter Meditation. It's similar to the chalkboard one except that, instead of trying to remember your thoughts, you let God transform them.

Guided meditation number 4: Divine filter

"Casting all your care upon him; for he careth for you" (1 Peter 5:7).

1. Make your usual preparations for meditation.

2. Close your eyes and imagine that you are sitting in a darkened room.

3. Now look up, in your mind's eye, and see an opening in the darkness, just above your head and about a foot or two in front of you. It is filled with thousands of tiny pinpoints of light. It is so PURE. It *is* purity; it is infinite wisdom; it is all-knowing, all-powerful goodness. It is God.
☐

4. Call Him by name; reach toward Him: *love* Him; feel His pure, sparkling love lighting that space above you. It is very

important to take as much time as you need, at this point, to really *feel* the presence of God hovering above you. ☐

5. Continue to bask in this loving, glistening awareness until a thought distracts you. Then *send the thought up through that shimmering space*. It doesn't matter whether the thought is pleasant, worrisome, or even evil. Send it forth. Feel it being transformed, purified, perfected, as it passes through the divine filter and out of your awarness. You will experience a glorious sense of release, of unburdening peace. ☐

6. Repeat this with each succeeding thought that arises during your meditation. ☐

After fifteen or twenty minutes of doing this, your body will feel almost weightless, there will be a tingling warmth in your heart, and your spirit will be soaring. But don't take my word for it. Try it. Running your worries through the one-pointedness of meditation has the same effect as running a comb through tangled hair. When you first start "combing," the worrisome thoughts pull and sting, but as you continue, the tangles smooth out. What happens is that, instead of repressing these thoughts, you hand them over to God for disposal.

I'm going to close this chapter on worry with a guided meditation that is a mosaic of scenes from my childhood, but you have been there, too. Don't try to call to mind places you've visited. Just relax and let your mind create its own scenes.

Guided meditation number 5: still waters

Relax comfortably in an easy chair and read the meditation slowly, experiencing it sentence by sentence. As with the other guided meditations in this book, read until you come to a box (☐); then stop, close your eyes, and experience what you've just read. Take several minutes at each stopping-place to let yourself really become part of the scene, seeing, hearing, feeling, merging into it, until you feel perfectly centered, balanced, deeply peaceful.

You are strolling along a country road on

a warm spring afternoon. There's no wind, only a feathery-light breeze stroking you. It soothes you and smooths away all feelings of tension and stress. ☐

For once, you're not in a hurry. There's nothing that has to be done today. Walk slowly down the road for a while, letting all the pressures inside of you evaporate into the weightless, buoyant air. ☐

Now you notice, off to your right, a beautiful green meadow, surrounded by thick, leafy cottonwoods. You decide to walk in the meadow for a while, so you leave the road and step into the soft green grass, which is about ankle-high. ☐

There's an old tree stump ahead of you, so you walk over, sit down on it, and take off your shoes and socks. The grass feels cool and soft under your feet. There aren't any stickers or sharp objects in this meadow, so you walk barefooted for a while, remembering the wonderful sense of freedom going barefooted gave you when you were a child. ☐

The sun is warm on your back and there are dainty little white and yellow wild flowers, swaying gently in the breeze, all around you. Can you see them? ☐

The scent of wild plum blossoms fills the air. You take a deep breath and savor nature's perfume as you continue to pad along in your bare feet. ☐

The musical sound of a meadowlark singing blends with the soft swish of the cottonwood leaves, and you have a wonderful feeling of peace and tranquility. You feel one with all of the things you're feeling and hearing and seeing. ☐

A monarch butterfly flutters lightly past you and you watch it as it flies off to your right and into a row of trees. You follow, and soon you're in the welcome shade of those trees, at the edge of a small, crystal-clear lake. ☐

As you gaze at the still, mirror-like water, you realize that it is a symbol of the calming, soothing, loving Christ-presence within you. Feel that Presence filling you, refreshing you, revitalizing you. ☐

Now you sit down on a large rock at the edge of the pond and put your feet in the water. It's lukewarm, and as it washes up over your feet and around your ankles, you feel soothed and comforted. Sit there for a while, feeling the warmth of the sun on your back and the coolness of the breeze in your hair. ☐

You notice, now, an egg-shaped stone on the ground by your left foot, so you pick it up and hold it in your hand. As you look down at the stone in your hand, you feel all of your worries, all of your troubled thoughts pouring out of you onto that little rock. Feel them going out of you, now, onto the rock. Just let them all go. It's all right. Just let them go. ☐

Now, throw the rock into the lake and watch it splash. Now it's sinking. Now it's completely gone. You watch the ripples from it slowly disappear, until the lake is smooth and calm again. ☐

The sun is starting to set now, and the whole sky is a soft, restful, cotton-candy pink. You put your shoes back on and walk slowly back through the meadow to the road, feeling serene and contented. Your while world is in perfect harmony. Take your time, and when you get back to the road, slowly open your eyes. ☐

Loving Christ, You are the calm center within me. You have led me beside the still waters and bathed me in Your peace. I have cast my worries, cares, burdens, into Your tranquil, healing waters. I am free, transformed by the renewing of my mind, serenely whole. Peace, peace, Prince of Peace, I praise Your name. Amen.

5

Improving human relationships through meditation

I have received permission from *Guideposts* magazine to reprint for you an article I wrote about my experience with a particularly difficult human relationship. I want to share it with you so that you can see that the meditations in this chapter are not mere idle exercises, but that they really do bring results.

Go ahead, hate me!*

"I'm Ka Yeung Kwan from Hong Kong. Just call me Kwan. I think English is a real bore. My main hobby is harassing stupid teachers, and English teachers are the stupidest of all—especially women."

It was the first day of classes at Kearney

*Reprinted from *Guideposts*, August, 1977, p. 10.

State College and I'd asked my freshman English students to tell a little about themselves. I hadn't been teaching in the department very long, and so, even though he said them jokingly, Kwan's words splattered against my ego like a rotten tomato.

The other students look embarrassed. During the rest of the period, Kwan snickered, mumbled under his breath, dropped books on the floor and squirmed in his seat.

Later, when I told my husband about it, he said, "You'd better crack down on him right now or you'll have trouble all semester." That night I prayed for strength to be firm. But then, as I was drifting off to sleep, the words, "See Christ in him," floated across my mind.

About halfway through the next class period, I heard a loud, "Ho-o-o hum! How boring!" It was Kwan, with a sly smirk on his face. I was ready to say, "If you're bored, Kwan, you can leave." But there was something in those dark eyes behind the thick glasses that stopped me. I ignored him and went on with my lecture.

After class, I noticed Kwan standing in

the doorway. I expected another smart remark, but he asked me a question about the literature we'd been discussing and walked back to my office with me. He now seemed a very intelligent, good-humored young man, and I was sure I'd have no more trouble with him.

I was wrong. In the classes that followed, Kwan seized every opportunity to practice his "hobby"—coming in late, making wisecracks, arguing with everything I said, interrupting other students. Yet every day he stayed after class, asking perceptive questions.

I couldn't figure Kwan out. He was really two different people—the childish, irritating boy who disrupted class, and the mature, thoughtful young man who was becoming my after-class friend.

His first essay was extremely well constructed, but it was sprinkled with obscene language, obviously intended to shock me. How could I see Christ in someone who used such unChristlike words?

One day after class, Kwan confided that all his life he'd been playing a game called never-let-anyone-know-you're-hurting. I understood, because I sometimes played that game, too.

I hoped that with our growing student-teacher friendship, the problem in class would dissolve. But if anything, it got worse. When we were studying the poem, "God's Grandeur," by Hopkins, Kwan monopolized the class discussion by arguing with the other students about their beliefs. It was upsetting to many of the students and doubly so to me. See Christ in Kwan? Was it really possible to "see Christ" in someone who wasn't even a Christian? *Maybe I should just squelch him, once and for all*, I thought.

Instead, I closed the class with a quotation from "Outwitted" by Edwin Markham and prefaced it with the words, "This is for Kwan."

He drew a circle that shut me out—
Heretic, rebel, a thing to flout.
But Love and I had the wit to win:
We drew a circle that took him in!

There was a warm silence in the classroom, and even Kwan seemed subdued.

After class, he said, "I can't understand you. Why don't you just give up on me?"

I felt like telling him how many times I *had* almost given up. I thought of telling him that I was trying to see Christ in him, but I didn't because, in spite of my efforts and prayers, I still couldn't quite do it. Christ, to me, was beautiful and loving and compassionate—all of the things Kwan's behavior showed *he* wasn't.

During our quiet talks, I had told Kwan about Christ's love, but I knew he was far from accepting it. Whenever I prayed about the problem, I seemed to get the same answer—not "Tell him about Christ," but "See Christ *in him*." Still, the more I tried, the harder he seemed to try to make me reject him.

Then came the essay in which Kwan wrote: "There are three kinds of teachers —those who are interesting but stupid, those who are intelligent but boring, and those who are both boring and stupid—like my English teacher." First I was angry, then hurt. Till now, I hadn't realized how much I really *cared* about this student. What about the friendship I thought we'd built? Did he really despise me so much?

I couldn't put a grade on his paper. When I handed it back without a mark on it, he waited for me after class.

"I'm sorry, Kwan," I said. "I can't play the game of never-let-anyone-know-I'm-hurting. I just lost." Then, to my horror and embarrassment, I started choking back tears. I hurried into my office and tried to eat my lunch, but I couldn't swallow. "Oh, God," I prayed, "why have I failed so badly with Kwan?"

I don't know how long I'd been sitting there, aching with rejection and failure, when Kwan walked in. Without a word he put a note on my desk and left. It said, "I did not know until now that you are just as vulnerable as I am. I meant the essay as a big, teasing joke. Instead, I hurt you, the only true friend I have . . . I've been rejected so often in my life that I've learned to protect myself by hurting other people first. But you wouldn't let me do it! You 'drew a circle that took me in.' If this has something to do with your Christ, then I think I'd like to know more about Him . . ."

Something to do with your Christ. Hurrying out of my office, I found Kwan standing near the stairs. Blind to the students all around us, we stood looking at each other, unable to speak. Then my insolent student took off his glasses, dried his eyes and handed me his handkerchief.

And in that moment, for the first time, to me Kwan *did* look Christlike.

Though the events in this story happened last year, the friendship between Kwan and me continues to grow. I don't have him in class anymore, but he often surprises me by dropping in on my classes, where he now *contributes* instead of disrupting. He often stops by my office just to talk, and our conversations turn easily to matters of the heart and spirit.

When you just don't want to forgive

Meditation can help us to see Christ in others, and I'll show you how this works in a minute. But first, let's admit that there are times when we don't *want* to forgive, when we'd rather *not* give up our resentments, when we feel we *need* our scapegoats. What then?

Hal Hill, Christian author and lecturer,

says that everyone has a "favorite stinker," and I think he's right. Often, we have very good reasons for resenting our "stinker." Maybe he or she has taken something that should rightfully be ours; or gossiped behind our backs; or embarrassed or belittled us, or stood in the way of our achievements; or deliberately hurt us or someone we love. Yet part of the reason most of us *need* a favorite stinker is so that we can direct our frustrations and hostilities *away from ourselves*. Very often, we fail to love others because we fail to love ourselves. When Christ said, "Love thy neighbor as thyself!" he implied that love for others is *based on* our ability to accept and love ourselves.

Erich Fromm, in his book, *The Art of Loving*, reminds us that self-love is not the same thing as selfishness. "Selfishness and self-love, far from being identical, are actually opposites. . . . It is true that selfish persons are incapable of loving others, but they are not capable of loving themselves either." So don't be afraid to love yourself. It is not a sign of selfishness, but is, in fact, a *prerequisite* for loving others. For that reason, the first meditation in this chapter on human relationships is directed not toward others but toward YOU.

Guided meditation number 6:
filling your vessel

Jesus told the woman at the well that, if she would but ask, He would give her "living water" (John 4:10). What is that living water but the pure, sparkling-clear love, which is God Himself? That is the living water that we seek when we meditate. But the only way you can carry that water to someone else is by first filling your own vessel.

At the still point between space and infinity, in the beginningless interval between time and eternity, a spring of living water flows. You could travel all over the world and never find it because it is beyond the physical senses. You could study a library of books and never learn of it, because it is beyond the limits of the human mind. It cannot be known. It can only be *experienced*.

God, who is Spirit, is the Source of the spring, and the opening is through a hole in your heart. You are the vessel that can hold the living water that pours forth from the ground of all Being.

Go into the silence now, find that spring, and fill your vessel with the freely given water of divine Love. Drink it in thirstily. Feel the water level rising in you. ☐

As you become aware of Spirit streaming into your heart, begin to pray, pausing at the end of each sentence to experience the infilling.

Clean my vessel, Lord. Wash away the sediment of guilt and unworthiness and false humility that muddies up your Water. ☐

Rinse away the crust of self-blame that coats my self-image. Help me to forgive myself so that the design you painted on my vessel may show through. ☐

Help me to so fill myself with Your love that there will be no room left for self-doubt or feelings of failure. ☐

I am your work of art. Show me that place in me where I am your beloved, perfectly created container, so that I may carry with me the image of who I can become. □

I ask these things not because of who I am but because of who You are—the inexhaustible source and substance of all Love. I can love myself only because You love me. I can forgive myself only because Christ bought my forgiveness with His life. I accept His gift. I accept Your grace. I am filled. Amen.

Go to your private, inner Spring every day to be filled, and soon you will find that your vessel can no longer contain all the water that flows in. Then let it spill over! You will find it impossible to hold back, anyway, once you have fully opened the valve in your heart.

Who will drink from your well?

With your newly filled vessel, it will be easy to "see Christ" in most people because the fountain of God's love feeds the spring in every person. But there will still probably be a few people that you'd rather not have drinking out of your pitcher. Right? Well, maybe something that helped me will help you, too. It's the realization that *you don't have to love the personality* of your favorite stinker(s). You don't have to love the way they look or act; you don't have to love the things they do or say. Just realizing this can be a tremendous relief. We are three-part beings, but only one of these parts is eternal, and that is our spirit. Our body dies and therefore is not part of our essential reality. Between body and spirit, there's that combination junkyard/garden that is called by various names. Whether you call it mind or personality or any other name, it too falls away eventually, so is not the essence of who we are. *The only element of your "favorite stinker" you have to love is his spirit*—that in him which partakes of God. How much easier this makes your task! There's no longer any reason to resist, is there? Now you can meditate on seeing Christ in him.

Radiating light meditation

1. Go to your meditation place, get comfortable, and relax.

2. Close your eyes and wait until you feel the presence of God surrounding you. Use the "Being of Light" meditation in Chapter 2, to become aware of the white light of Christ within you.

3. Then call to mind the person you need to learn to love. Picture him or her as vividly as you can.

4. Realize, in your deep consciousness, that underneath all the negative personality stuff, this person too has within him the same being of light. True, he may not be aware of it and he certainly isn't manifesting it, but it is there nevertheless.

5. As you feel the soft white light glowing within your own heart, visualize a similar circle of light radiating from the center of the other person's chest.

6. Let the rays from *your* being of light extend outward in a clear beam, till it makes contact with the light in that other person. Hold. Hold. Continue to hold the contact until you feel something like an electrical current passing between you and the image of the other person.

7. Then release him and give thanks.

8. When you meet the person in real life, try to recreate in your mind that

transmission of light. Let it pierce through all the external feelings, actions, and words, to the very spirit within him, which is from God. As I learned from Kwan, it doesn't even matter whether or not the person is a Christian. Christ died for *all* men and He lives in all, whether or not they acknowledge Him. You will probably have to repeat this meditation many times before you will begin to feel the love *manifesting*, in your relationship, but if you stick with it, it will do just that—and more. The change in the way you see that other person will bring about a change in the way he responds to you. Psychologists have demonstrated this in controlled studies; you can *experience* it.

And there's a bonus! Once you've managed to "see Christ" in one difficult person, you will begin to meet Him everywhere! This has been true for me. Once I had found Him in Kwan, I began to "see" that white light flowing from the inner being of: a lady in our church who had always seemed cold and aloof to me; a relative with whom I'd had strained relations; a dentist who had seemed gruff and unfeeling, and many others. The rewards are tangible and active and worth your best efforts.

If you are lonely or shy

Maybe your problem is not so much in handling difficult relationships or overcoming resentments. It may be that you are lonely, or shy, or lacking friends. How can meditation help you?

Dan Custer, author of *The Miracle of Mind Power*, says: "Everyone gravitates toward that person or place which is most pleasant. . . . Attracting people to you is a mental operation. Liking and loving people is something which goes on in your mind; so when others like you and respond to you, it is the result of a certain state of mind *within you*" (italics added).

Furthermore, Custer notes that "We are now told by scientists that each one of us is actually a radio transmitter as well as receiver; that certain cells of our bodies and certain cells of the brain are transmitting sets and others are receiving stations. We certainly do set up definite mental vibrations at the place where we think and the result is that a corresponding something happens in the body, the affairs and even in the thinking and acting of other people."

So how can we learn to send out the kind of signals that will draw people to us? First of all, those signals will have to be positive and not negative; we will have to transmit love signals. As we discussed in the beginning of this chapter, you can't carry love to others if your own vessel is empty. Your vessel may be empty because no one filled it for you as a child. You may have felt rejected or unloved. If that's the case, you *could* choose to go on blaming and resenting those who failed you. That would be one way of filling your vessel, but that would only be packing it with mud. OR— you could look to God for the love you feel deprived of. This will not mean getting love from God *instead* of from others. Once your vessel is filled, others will come to drink from it.

So use the vessel-filling meditation at the beginning of every day. It is especially important for you to fill your vessel just before going out among people. If you continue to do this, you will unconsciously begin sending out positive signals which will draw others to you. I am a rather shy person myself, so I know what it's like to feel isolated in a crowd. But since I've been meditating regularly, I find that I feel good about myself most of the time and this good feeling spills over, making it easier for me to open myself to others.

Special relationships

If there's a particular person you want to establish a close relationship with, use the radiating light meditation, holding steady the connection between your light and his or hers.

How can this have any effect? Emerson said, "There is one mind common to all individual men." C. G. Jung called this mind the "collective unconscious." Call it what you will, I have no doubt that a thought at one point in this universal mind can and does create a response at another point. I don't know if that is the explanation of why the radiating light meditation works or not. I only know it does work. It has worked in my own life and it can work in yours.

Here is a poem by Richard Bowen that may give you some new insight into this matter of human relationships.

Please hear what I'm *not* saying
    Don't be fooled by me.
Don't be fooled by the face I wear.
For I wear a mask, a thousand masks,
    masks that I'm afraid to take off, and
    none of them are me.

Pretending is an art that's second
    nature with me, but don't be fooled,
    for God's sake don't be fooled.
I give you the impression that I'm
    secure,
that all is sunny and unruffled with me,
within as well as without,
that confidence is my name and
    coolness my game.
That the water's calm and I'm in
    command,
and that I need no one.
But don't believe me.
Please.

My surface may seem smooth, but my

surface is my mask, my ever-varying and ever-concealing mask.
Beneath lies no smugness, no complacence.
Beneath dwells the real me in confusion, in fear, in aloneness.
But I hide this.
I don't want anybody to know it.
I panic at the thought of my weakness and fear being exposed.

That's why I frantically create a mask to hide behind, a nonchalant, sophisticated façade,
to help me pretend,
to shield me from the glance that knows.
But such a glance is precisely my salvation.
My only salvation.
And I know it . . .

Only you can call me to aliveness.
Each time you're kind, and gentle, and encouraging, each time you try to understand because you really care, my heart begins to grow wings,

very small wings, very feeble wings,
but wings.

With your sensitivity and sympathy,
and your power of understanding,
you can breathe life into me. I want
you to know that.
I want you to know how important you
are
to me, how you can be a creator of the
person that is me if you choose to.
Please choose to.

You alone can break down the wall
behind
which I tremble.
You alone can remove my mask,
You alone can release me from my
shadow-
world of panic and uncertainty,
from my lonely prison.

So do not pass me by.
It will not be easy for you.
A long conviction of worthlessness
builds strong walls.
The nearer you approach me, the
blinder

121

I
may strike back.
It's irrational, but despite what the
books say about man, I am
irrational.

I fight against the very thing that I cry
out for.
But I am told that Love is stronger than
strong walls, and in this lies my hope.
My only hope. Please try to beat down
these walls with firm hands, but
with gentle hands—for a child is
very sensitive.

Who am I, you may wonder? I am
someone
you know very well.
For I am every man you meet and I am
every woman you meet.

If we could only grasp the truth in this
poem, we could see Christ in every person.
For behind the ever-changing masks each
person wears, a living spirit breathes.
Beneath the false veneer each heart puts
on, a shining vessel opens wide its thirsty
mouth.

The guided meditation that concludes this chapter is special to me because empty churches and candles are two of my favorite things. They seem to come together at some place in me where love moves. I hope I can transmit this love to you.

Guided meditation number 7: candlelighting

Have you ever been alone in a church at night? If you have, you know the soft whisper of reverence that comes over you when you go in and close the door, shutting out the busy world so you can be alone in the stillness with your God.

Go to that church or chapel now, in your imagination. Let the filled silence fall on your tired heart. Soak warm peace into your soul. □

Now become aware of that candle-glow you've learned to light in your heart. Feel it as God's love, warming, soothing, healing. □

Reach into your heart and grasp the candle,

holding it in front of you as you walk down the aisle. ☐

Kneel before the altar and ask God to bless the light of love you hold in your hands. ☐

Receive his blessing. ☐
Now slowly walk back down the aisle, stopping at each pew to light from *your* taper the candle of each person you want to bless. Include the difficult people in your life as well as your loved ones. Take your time, and when you reach the back of the church, give thanks and place the candle back in your heart. ☐

Blessed Christ, light of the world, ignite in my heart the love that no hostile winds can extinguish. Make my candle bright enough to show the beauty, and soft enough to hide the faults, of those it shines upon. And when my candle begins to flicker, lead me back to Your kindling light. Amen.

6

Establishing harmony in the physical body through meditation

IT was late on a gray afternoon a few days before Christmas. I'd spent the morning in the dentist's chair and the afternoon Christmas shopping, so when John walked in from school and begged me to make Christmas cookies with him, all I could do was moan.

"Whatsa matter, Mom?"

"Oh, nothing much. It's just that I'm so tired and I can feel a headache coming on and . . . " Before I could finish my sentence, he interrupted me with, "Oh no. Quick! Go meditate!"

Well, it isn't really that simple, and meditation is certainly not a cure-all, but John's reaction that day was based on history—mine. All my adult life, I'd had frequent severe headaches. I'd gone to various medical specialists and tried everything from ice packs to heating pads to pills to allergy shots to counseling, but it gradually occurred to me that my headaches were becoming less frequent and less severe. As the weeks went by, I began to see that, *as long as I was meditating regularly*, I simply didn't have my usual disabling headaches. I might have missed the *reason* for the change except that, now and then I'd let my meditation go for several days and wham! I'd end up in bed with a migraine.

Now this is just *my* experience and I'm not presenting it as evidence for meditation as a cure for headaches. If you have headaches, or any other physical problem, by all means see your doctor and follow his instructions. But my experience with headache *does* seem to be in keeping with laboratory evidence that indicates that meditation reduces anxiety and bodily tension.

Within the past few years, the scientific community has become intensely interested in studying the physical effects of meditation, and the results of a large number of controlled studies have been published. The evidence is clear that definite relationships do exist between serious meditation and certain physical conditions.

Physical benefits of meditation

Probably the most extensive research has been done by a group headed by Dr. Herbert Benson, of the Harvard Medical School, a cardiologist who is specializing in hypertension. Basically, meditation seems to bring about a state of deep physical relaxation coupled with a highly alert mental state. The physical changes include:

lowered rate of metabolism
slowing of the heartbeat
decrease in rate and volume of
    respiration
decrease in blood lactate level
increased skin resistance
changes in brainwave patterns

All of these physical signs bear witness to a remarkable state of relaxation that is measurably *different* from quiet sitting, sleep, or hypnosis. It would seem that, in such an extremely relaxed state, the mind would become sluggish, but this is not the case. In fact, the opposite effect has been noted by researchers. For instance, when asked to depress a key on signal, meditators averaged a 30 percent faster response that non-meditators. "In other words, the practitioners of meditation not only enjoy a habitual freedom from anxiety and restlessness, but they are also more alert and their response is faster."

Long-range effects

In addition to these changes that occur *during* meditation, there are also some long-range therapeutic effects that take place among those who meditate regularly. Dr. Benson, in his work with hypertension, also conducted some controlled studies of people who had high blood pressure. The patients meditated twice daily, and their blood pressures were measured every two weeks for at least nine weeks. The measurements were taken at random times of the day, but not *during* meditation. The results showed that:

During the premeditation [control] period, the subjects' systolic blood pressures averaged 140 to 150 millimeters of mercury. [Systolic pressure is the measure of the highest component of blood pressure.] After nine weeks of regular elicitation of the relaxation response [meditation], this average dropped into the range of 130 to 140 millimeters. Their diastolic pressures [the lowest component of blood pressure] averaged 90 to 95 millimeters during the control period and dropped into the range of 85 to 90 millimeters by the ninth week of meditation. These decreases reflect a statistically significant change in blood pressure, from what is considered the borderline hypertensive range to the normal range of blood pressure.

However, this does not mean that you should put off having your blood pressure checked or stop taking your medication because you have started meditating. Dr. Benson makes this very clear, as he concludes his study in this way:

However, no matter how encouraging these

initial results appear to be, no person should treat himself for high blood pressure by regularly eliciting the relaxation response [meditation].

Decreased dependence on alcohol, drugs, and cigarettes

Because meditation seems to be effective in draining off excessive stress, those who practice it regularly usually find that they have less need for alcohol, drugs, and cigarette smoking. In a recent investigation, 1,862 individuals completed a questionnaire in which they reported a marked decrease in hard-liquor intake, drug abuse, and cigarette smoking after they had begun the practice of meditation.

Increased energy and sense of well-being

In addition to the measurable physical changes brought about through meditation, there are certain subjective sensations that you will probably notice after you've been meditating regularly for a while. One is a general, overall feeling of well-being. I don't really know how to describe this, and it is probably a little different for each person. What I feel is a kind of *lightness*, an airy sensation that sort of "floats" through me during the day. My body movements feel graceful, too, as if they were keeping time to some internal rhythm. Most meditators experience an increase in energy too. My family first noticed this in me when I started bouncing up our basement steps without my usual two or three rest stops on the way up! I just *feel* better most of the time.

Another thing I've noticed is that there is an awakening of the senses. Colors seem brighter; music goes all the way into me; I can run my finger over a piece of wood and feel the grain of it in my toes; the sweetness of an orange is as satisfying now as a chocolate sundae used to be. All of these things add up to increased feelings of well-being that go hand-in-glove with the newer, fresher awareness of Christ's presence in all the little and big moments of my life. I think you'll discover what I mean as you begin to meditate regularly.

Emotions and health

We all know about the close relationship between our habitual state of mind and our health. We know, intellectually, at least, that many physical ailments result from tension, emotional upsets, buried resentments, fears, and guilts. This is *not* the same as saying, "It's all in your head." The illness is real; the pain is real; the misery is real. It doesn't do any good at all for someone to say, "Snap out of it." You *would* if you *could*, for heaven's sake!

One way to turn "would" into "could" is to break the fear-worry-tension-illness spiral by a combining of physical relaxation techniques and meditation. Edmund Jacobson, in his book, *You Must Relax*, points out that physiological tests "indicate that when you imagine or recall about anything, you tense muscles somewhere, as if you were actually looking or speaking or doing something." He maintains that, when you consciously relax these muscular tensions, your ability to hold onto negative emotions is greatly diminished. You can prove this to yourself. Sit still for three minutes, thinking of someone or something that makes you very angry. What happens? Your fists may begin to clench, your jaws tighten, your neck muscles tense up, your stomach starts to churn around, your breathing may become faster, your lips press tightly together, etc. You just can't be really angry or fearful or emotionally upset at the same time that you are completely relaxed. It's impossible!

So you've got a choice. You can either say, "I can't relax because I'm upset," or you can flip that over and say, "I can't be upset because I'm so relaxed." You must consciously choose the second way or the first will win by default. Of course, you can't just say, "I *will* relax," and expect to have results. So how do you make it work? Regular meditation is the only way I know to reverse the spiral, and by regular I mean at least twice a day every day. When you give yourself a chance to drain off stress two or three times a day through meditation, you will find that you have *reinherited your own body*. It can no longer be kicked around by external events beyond your control. Instead, it will take its orders from that calm, balanced center within, where *you* are master.

Besides benefiting your health by relaxing you, meditation can also give you increased energy. I know of no better description of the relationship between meditation and energy than the following: "They that wait upon the Lord [a perfect definition of meditation] shall renew their strength; they shall mount up with wings as eagles; they shall run, and not be weary; and they shall walk, and not faint" (Isaiah 40:31).

I will now give you a guided meditation that will help you to become *aware* of this omnipresence of divine energy and its availability to you. In this meditation, I'm going to ask you to imagine something, but I want you to know that, even though you cannot see it with your physical eyes, what I ask you to visualize really exists. You cannot see energy, and yet there is not the tiniest space in the universe that is void of it. The late Donald Hatch Andrews, who was professor of chemistry at Atlantic University in Florida, gives us this startling fact: "Our physical eyes are capable of perceiving less than *one-millionth part* of all the radiation around us." Andrews makes this dazzlingly clear in his book, *The Symphony of Life*, in which he writes:

Close your eyes for a moment. I have a wand. Now look about you. The room is ablaze with dazzling light. The chairs, the tables—are prismatic crystals, sparkling with a thousand shades of red, yellow, green and blue such as you have never in your life seen before. Your clothes are on fire with a million microscopic flames. Your bodies are shining ruby, emerald, and sapphire. The air itself sparks as if millions of miniature meteors are darting all about you.

Professor Andrews's description is not a dream or hallucination. Even though our physical eyes are not equipped to see this amazing display that is going on all around us at this very moment, it *is* happening nonetheless. Try to keep this in mind as you do the meditation.

Guided meditation number 8:
sparkling mist

1. Begin by doing the relaxation exercises described on pages 56-62 of Chapter 3. ☐

2. Sit down and get *centered* by leaning first to one side, then the other, and then back to the center until you feel perfectly balanced. Then do the same thing by leaning forward, then backward, and back to center. Finally, repeat this centering procedure with your head. You should now have a feeling of perfect balance, quiet equanimity. ☐

3. Now close your eyes and begin to visualize a white mist, composed of millions of tiny particles of energy glistening like diamonds. Let the mist surround you, extending outward several feet on all sides of you, rising above your head and below your feet. It is a shaft of bright and shining light that comes through the ceiling of the room, like a waterfall, shimmering, with all those radiant specks alive and dancing. Think of this as the great life force, the cosmic energy, the spiritual substance of

the universe, the Holy Spirit. Experience it now. ☐

4. Then take a long, slow, deep breath, drawing this life-giving Spirit substance into your lungs. Hold your breath for about five seconds as you feel it entering into the tiny air sacs of your lungs and passing from there into your circulatory system. Then let your breathing return to normal. ☐

5. Inhale again and feel the sparkling mist spreading upward from your lungs into your throat, your mouth, your nose, your ears and eyes. Feel it dancing among the cells of your brain, vitalizing, sharpening, quickening your mind. ☐

6. Each time you take a breath, become aware of your heartbeat pumping the energy mist into a different part of your body. Feel it flowing down your arms into your fingertips until your hands begin to tingle . . . ☐

coursing through all of the organs in your abdomen, cleansing, purifying . . . ☐

pulsing into your legs, feet, toes, warming, restoring . . . ☐

7. Draw in another breath and feel the mist streaming into all of the tiny blood vessels, veins, and capillaries of your body, livening every cell, tingling every inch of your skin. ☐

8. Bathe in this shimmering light of Spirit for as long as you wish, continuing to inhale it, being renewed and invigorated by it. ☐

9. Return to it whenever you need to renew your strength

Healing effects of meditation

In addition to its relaxing and energizing effects, which help to *maintain* health, meditation can also be used to promote healing. Time and again, when Jesus healed, he said, "Thy faith hath made thee whole." But maybe you've prayed night and day for healing and you are not one bit better. You have faith in God. You believe in His ability to make you whole, but you're still sick. What's wrong? It's hard to *pray believing* when your joints feel as if they're on fire or your head is pounding or your ulcer is biting. It's really very hard to *know* clear down in the marrow of your bones, that you are being healed, and that's the kind of faith it takes. So how can you acquire that unshakable inner knowing? If faith is "the substance of things hoped for, the evidence of things not seen" (Hebrews II:1), maybe what you need for your healing is *substance* and *evidence*. There is a form of meditation, called programmed visualization, that gives you substance and evidence in the form of very detailed images of healing and wholeness to picture that will help you to pray believing. Probably the most dramatic application of this type of meditation is being made by Dr. Carl Simonton of Fort Worth, Texas. Dr. Simonton is a radiation therapist who has had notable success with a meditation-like visualization procedure in the treatment of cancer patients. He described his approach in *The Journal of Transpersonal Psychology* (No. 1, 1975):

We teach our patients a technique which

we call relaxation and visualization. You might call it biofeedback without a machine, meditation, autogenic training. There are lots of names for it, but it is a basic relaxation technique in which the patients are told to visualize their disease, their treatment and their body's own immune mechanisms (we call them white blood cells to make it simple), acting on that disease. We tell them to do this three times a day, every day.

Simonton has found that patients who "follow instructions implicitly and are enthusiastic about getting better show marked relief of symptoms and dramatic improvement of condition." Many have fully recovered.

Other physicians are using meditation-visualization with a variety of illnesses. The book, *Be Well*, by Mike Samuels, M.D. and Hal Bennett, gives examples of such meditations. For instance, "If you have a virus infection you might imagine the virus as tiny dots on a blackboard and then imagine yourself erasing those dots." Or, if you have sinus trouble, picture "the tubes opening and the fluid draining out from the sinuses like a sink unclogging." Or, if you have a headache, "imagine you have a hole in your head near the area of your headache. As you exhale your breath imagine that the pain is going out through that hole and is colored a murkey muddy color."

Visualizations of this kind deal with a healing *process*, but another way to approach the problem is by visualizing the *desired final state*. In other words, seeing yourself recovered and healthy. This way may be best, especially in situations involving healing processes you may not fully understand.

The following is a guided meditation of a general nature that is good for developing and/or maintaining a good state of health. If you have specific health problems, you will of course want to follow whatever treatment your doctor prescribes. In addition, you may invent your own programmed visualization-meditation, starting with this general one and adapting it to fit your specific needs. Your visualizations will have more substance if you find some pictures of healing images that relate to your problem. These may

141

come from medical books, or biology and science textbooks from the library, where you will find pictures of healthy organs, and body parts, contrasting pictures of sick versus healthy organs, and pictures depicting the healing process. You will probably find drawings of such things as white blood cells shown engulfing disease bacteria. Visualizing this kind of sequence can give substance and evidence to your faith and make it easier to pray believing.

Guided meditation number 9: heal yourself

As in previous guided meditations, I advise you to tape-record this if at all possible, or to have someone else read it to you as you follow through with it.

Part I: body harmony

1. This meditation may be done either by itself or as a continuation of the energy meditation. If you have just done the energy meditation, you have been

breathing deeply and you are now filled with the healing mist of the life force. If you are starting your meditation here, take five slow, deep breaths, filling your lungs to capacity and then emptying them as completely as possible. ☐

2. Let your eyes gently close, and then become aware of your breathing as it returns to normal. Begin to count your breaths. Count to four and begin again. Do this several times and you will notice that your breathing becomes more shallow, more regular. Say to yourself, "My breathing is calm and regular." ☐

3. Now become aware of your heart beating. If you can't feel it, you may need to place your fingers on the pulse at your wrist or throat. Say to yourself, "My heartbeat is calm and regular." As you repeat this sentence, think of the blood circulating life-giving oxygen and food to every cell in your body, swallowing up impurities and carrying them away. Continue in this way until you experience the deep and steady *rhythm* of your body, perfectly synchronized, stable, constant. ☐

4. Mentally tune in to the ebb and flow of your system's hormonal and digestive tides as they operate in perfect harmony throughout your body. Say to yourself, "All of the organs of my body are functioning exactly as they should." Feel this process as an inner dance, with every dancer in step, and the whole company projecting a graceful symmetry. ☐

Part II: touch of spirit

But you are more, much more, than just a body. If you could peel away all the layers of skin and flesh and bones and organs you call your self, there would still be something left that's you. If you could cut through level after level of your personality characteristics, the programmed *stuff* you've thought of as "who you are"— underneath all that you'd still find an untouched something that is the real YOU. There would still be a self that you would recognize as your own unique spirit, a spark of the divine that is untouched by illness, pain, disease, or even death. If you can bring your consciousness to a mind-space that touches that deepest transcendental self, you will know the truth about yourself, which is: that you are always and forever WHOLE.

. . . substance . . . evidence . . . faith . . . knowing . . . wholeness. In this way, you will be healed.

So now, if you're ready, let's see if we can touch that place by an awareness-expanding visualization that will take you beyond yourself.

  1. Move around a little in your chair if necessary, and get relaxed and comfortable. ☐

2. Gradually feel your body becoming lighter . . . and lighter . . . and lighter. ☐

3. Let your physical being pass completely out of your awareness now, so that you are conscious only of your spiritual self, which is who you really are underneath all of the perishables. ☐

4. Now let this lighter-than-air self float

upward, passing through the ceiling of your home or building, drifting weightlessly and effortlessly above your neighborhood, above your city, until you are high enough to see for miles around you. Relax. Rest there now, reclining on a cloud. ☐

5. Now look down from your cloud and see the bustle and stir and hum of busy activity below. See the people rushing and resting and fighting, embracing and laughing and crying, aching with pain and shouting for joy. Accept all of it. It's all all right. ☐

6. Soar higher now, and look down on the rivers and lakes and mountains and plains and know in your heart that "It is good." ☐

7. Rise still higher until the earth becomes a gleaming turquoise ball surrounded by the royal blue velvet of outer space. ☐

8. Now look upward and outward and you will see an area of soft white light glowing in the distance. Without straining, let yourself move comfortably and easily closer

and closer to the light. Closer now. Closer . Travel into the light. Let your light merge with its light. ☐

9. Rest quietly, calmly in this light-space . . . until you hear the words, "Your faith has made you whole." Wait and listen. Be still . . . still . . . still . . . you will hear the words. Wait and listen . . . be still . . . wait . . . listen . . . ☐

10. After you have received the blessing, visualize yourself moving slowly back through space to the earth, your city, your house, your chair, your body made whole.

Light of the world, Spirit of my spirit, breath of my life, I have touched the hem of Your garment and You have made me whole. Praise. Praise. I praise Your name forever. Amen.

7

Handling emotions through meditation

YOU are walking alone in a dark forest at night, when you suddenly smell smoke. You look back and see tongues of fire leaping toward you with unbelievable speed. Panic-stricken, you begin to run . . . faster and faster, but the flames gain on you. Heat sears your back; smoke fumes choke you; you run . . . harder . . . faster . . . and now, suddenly, you see a clearing ahead that appears to be a body of water. You rush toward it with your heart hammering in your throat, only to find that it is a pit, inky black and hundreds of feet deep. Behind you are the flames; ahead is the pit. There's no way out. You open your mouth and try to scream but you can't make a sound!

Well, of course that was just a made-up nightmare, but it can serve as a rather dramatic symbol of the kind of double bind negative emotions can lead us into. Anger.

Fear. Jealousy. Grief. Resentment. Guilt, Loneliness. Sorrow. Self-pity. They are all as real and as painful as tongues of fire. If we live with them, they will surely burn us and those around us and shrivel up our ability to enjoy life. On the other hand, if we try to run away from them through alcohol or drugs and just by denying they exist (repression), we end up falling into the black pit of depression.

Here the comparison with the nightmare ends, because we don't have to be trapped by our emotions. There *is* a way out. We don't have to go forward into the pit or backward into the flame. We can go *upward* through meditation. It's the only way I know for handling negative emotions without burning ourselves or others, without running away, without repressing. What happens to the emotion, then? When you bring a painful emotion into the inner Light through meditation, holding it there in the Presence, it simply disintegrates. You begin to *resee* the situation in a new and overturning way and you *rise above* that emotion.

Dr. Daniel Goleman, a Harvard

psychologist who investigated meditation as a means of coping with stress, writes:

> People who meditate have long recognized in themselves and in fellow meditators marked improvement of their psychological state and psychosomatic disorders . . . Even someone who has just begun to meditate regularly can notice that immediately after each meditation he is not so likely to respond to people and situations in a tense way —he is relaxed, and can take things as they come. With prolonged practice of meditation, this relaxed stance toward life's vicissitudes pervades the meditator's day. He finds himself reacting with equanimity where once he would have gotten angry, paranoid, envious, greedy, titillated, or whatever reaction his particular personality makes him susceptible to.

You'll find, after you've been meditating regularly for some time, that you can *choose* how you're going to react to a particular situation. You are no longer a leaf blown helplessly about by the winds of external events. You are a bird who *uses* those same winds for *lift*. "Nothing can work me damage except myself," said St. Bernard. "The harm that I sustain I carry about with me, and am never a real sufferer but by my own fault." When you are in control of your life in the deep inner center of your being, you can choose *not* to suffer.

Cleaning out emotional debris

So how can meditation help us to avoid carrying around all our negative emotions? Just as we need to brush our teeth every day to keep them from accumulating tartar and decaying, we also need to purify our inner self daily so we will not accumulate emotional debris that will rot out our souls. One way of doing this is to use the Divine Filter meditation given in Chapter 4.

This way has worked so well for me that I can tell a very distinct difference in my overall mood on the days that I miss doing it. One day last fall, I had a writing deadline to meet and a stack of essays to grade, but I couldn't seem to concentrate on either task. My mind just kept returning to a chance remark my brother had made the day before. For some reason, it seemed to stir up some old buried guilts and resentments from my childhood. I finally gave up trying to concentrate and went out to rake leaves. As I crunched around out there in the brown grass and brittle leaves, it occurred to me that trees would die in the winter if they didn't get rid of their old leaves, because the energy drain would be so great. It was like the energy drain *I* was feeling because I was clinging to old hurts. What I needed to do was to let go of the dead leaves in my life! I sat down right out there under the sycamore tree and started doing the Divine Filter meditation, and as I passed the disturbing thoughts up through that sparkling space, old wounds started dropping away like falling leaves. Then, with a new surge of energy, I went back to my desk and had no more trouble concentrating on my work.

Have you tried blessing it?

Another thing that helps is to mentally go over your day each night before going to sleep. Whenever your mind hits upon something that stirs a negative emotion, *bless it*. The Bible says that "All things work together for good to them that love the Lord" (Romans 8:28). The amazing thing is—it's true! All you have to do is to stop struggling with your problems, and instead, bless them and *command them to yield the good that is in them*. Take God up on His promise. Make Him prove it! Say, believing . . .

"*I bless this despair*, knowing that if I can hang onto this 'end of the rope' just a little longer, God will use it to pull me back up.

"*I bless this guilt feeling*, knowing that God can take any bad thing I may have done and bring good out of it, if I ask His help. I know, too, that He wants me to forgive myself, just as He forgives me.

"*I bless this fear*, knowing that it can teach me to take hold of God's hand in the dark.

"*I bless this bad luck*, knowing that this very act of blessing can open inner doors that

153

may have been keeping my good from reaching me.

"*I bless this time of material lack*, knowing that I can use it to reassess my sense of values and decide what is really important in my life.

"*I bless this frustration*, knowing that doing so will untangle my knotted emotions so I can concentrate freely on my problem.

"*I bless these hurt feelings*, knowing that they can show me what a stagnant pond self-pity is. Blessing will help me to forgive, and get me quickly back to the living waters where love moves.

"*I bless this grief*, knowing that it can lead me to the still-open crack in the black door that slammed when my loved one died.

"*I bless this doubt*, knowing that I can use it to stretch and freshen my faith.

"*I bless this failure*, knowing that I can use it as yeast to give rise to future successes."
Whatever the causes of the negative

feelings are, bless them and command them to "work together for good" in your life. Do this each night before you fall asleep, and you will be surprised at the transformation that will begin to take place in you and in the events of your life.

Practicing nonresponse

You can also immunize yourself against excessive negative emotions by systematically introducing them into your mind during meditations planned for that purpose. What you do is to use your imagination to practice nonresponse to situations that would normally upset you.

Get relaxed and comfortable. Choose a Logos (see Chapter 3) that has worked well for you in the past and begin meditating with it. After about ten minutes of meditation, when you're feeling quite calm, imagine yourself in a stress-producing situation (e.g. the boss is ranting and raving at you) *but* see yourself sitting quietly and calmly, composed and meditating, through it all. Watch the boss looking ridiculous because you are not responding in the least.

Practice this often, and you'll soon find yourself responding with equanimity when such situations arise in the external world. It's also an excellent way to prepare for a dreaded interview or frightening public appearance or the like.

The preceding methods are all preventive measures, long-term methods for keeping your emotional machinery from getting clogged. But what about those times when you're already in the throes of a painful emotion? What can you do then? Here are three very specific, realistic techniques that can help you.

The unattached observer

One reason negative emotions can be so painful is because we try to deny them, squelch them, push them back. We don't want to see such ugly things in ourselves. But if we can come to realize that *we are not our emotions*, then we can look at them objectively and take control. How do we go about separating ourselves from our emotions? One way is to have a "stare-down."

Find a place where you can be alone and undisturbed for about fifteen minutes. Have pen and paper and mirror handy.

1. *Name the emotion you're feeling.* Let's say you're angry at your sister-in-law for scolding your child. So you write, *Anger.* Be careful not to say "I am" in connection with the emotion. Instead of saying, "I am angry," say "I feel anger." This is an important distinction because *you are not the emotion.*

2. Ask yourself: *where* do I feel it? Is the feeling in the pit of my stomach? In my chest? My throat? Behind my eyes? Where? The answer, "All over" is not allowed. You *must* locate it exactly.

3. Now go inside and focus your attention on that area and then just *let it hurt. Feel* the emotion to the fullest. Don't cover it over, hide from it, ignore it, or talk yourself out of it. Just let it hurt as *much* as it can. It's all right. You are just observing.

4. Now, study that pain. What does it feel *like*? A dull knife? A meat grinder? A vice? Think up your own metaphor that really describes the pain of that emotion.

5. Examine it some more. How big is it? What shape is it? What color?

6. *Symbolize* it in some way by drawing a picture of how it feels or describing it in writing or making a sound that echoes the way it feels. In other words, *objectify it*. Change it from a dark shadowy threat to something tangible. For instance, you might take a red crayon and draw a sharp flame or a black pen to make an ugly spider, or you might just take a pencil and scribble all over a piece of paper. This gets the emotion outside of you.

7. Now ask yourself: who is it that has been studying this emotion? It will become obvious that the observer is separate from the emotion. *You are not that emotion*.

8. Feel it some more. Go ahead. It has been said that suffering is grace. Suffer, then, but watch yourself doing it. *Who* is doing the watching?

9. Moan and groan and cry if you feel like it, but *listen* to the sounds. *Who* is doing the listening?

10. Now, notice the tremendous amount of energy your body has generated through experiencing this emotion. Your heart is probably beating faster, your blood pressure is likely to be up, your muscles

are toned up. *What constuctive thing can you think of to do with this energy bonus?*

11. Don't let go of the emotion until it has given you a gift, until you've taken all you can from it. *Use* it.

If you will meet your unpleasant emotions head-on in this way, you'll find that they really have no power over you. Psychological pain is deepened when we fight it or fear it. But when we allow it to happen, when we are able to look at it objectively, it loses its threat-power.

Chanting dissipates emotions

Another good on-the-spot treatment for painful emotions is chanting. This, too, is a form of meditation. You can chant the words of a prayer or a psalm, or you can just use the vowel sounds. Here's the way that works well for me.

Start with the "ah" sound. Open your mouth and just begin to make the sound. Then raise and lower the pitch several times and you'll soon find the pitch that touches the place in you where it hurts. You'll know when you find it. It'll just *feel* right. Now

159

just keep chanting "ah" on that note, take a breath whenever you feel the need. Increase and decrease the loudness, letting your voice swell till you feel the vibration filling your whole chest cavity. It will feel as though a firmly massaging hand is giving you a healing internal rub-down. You know the relief you feel when you massage your aching feet. Chanting massages your aching heart. After you've done this for a while, you may want to vary the pitch, moving up and down the scale and then coming back to the pitch that touches the ache. Or you may use a different vowel sound, or several in sequence, such as: ah, oh, oo, ee, ay, etc. In this way, you can vary the chanting procedure in any way that feels good to you. Chanting is especially suitable for people who live alone or work alone or those who have the house to themselves during the daytime, but it's also a good in-the-car technique that you can use on the way to work, to the store, or on a trip, Once, after a trying experience in a nearby town, I chanted most of the fifty miles home. I didn't have much voice left when I got there, but I felt absolutely invigorated, and there was not a trace of painful emotion left in me.

Meditation in times of severe stress

When I first started reading and studying about meditation, it seemed to me that the teachers and writers on the subject claimed too much for it. I had doubts about whether or not meditation really *could* effect such important changes in a person's life. When I started applying it to my Christian faith, though, I could see that meditation was not a miracle-worker but a way of opening the channel between God and the individual human being. Even then, I had reservations about it. Was it just a mind-trick that created a new illusion? If so, I knew it would not bear the test of time. It's so easy for new ideas to catch fire, but so often, after the first glow wears off, the fire goes out. Because I have known these doubts, and because you may also feel them, I am going to tell you about the experience that answered these questions for me for all time.

It is very difficult for me to talk about it,

but I feel that, if you have read this far in my book, you and I share a common ground and I can talk to you as I would to a close friend.

One Sunday in 1976, less than a week before Christmas, our oldest son, Paul, was getting ready for an important date. I had helped him pick out a necklace for his pretty little girl friend, Rita. It was her eighteenth birthday, and Paul had been so eager to find just the right gift. He left the house at 5:30 to pick her up for the dinner date. An hour later, Rita was dead and Paul was in critical condition in the intensive care unit at the hospital. His car had gone off the road at the edge of Kearney Lake, overturned, and struck a tree, which tore off the whole top of the car. Rita was killed instantly. Paul had a severe concussion, serious internal injuries, and deep facial cuts. For three days, he remained in a coma, hovering between life and death. We were allowed into intensive care only five minutes of every hour. The rest of the time we sat, in a state of utter shock, in a nearby waiting room. Sometime during that first night, I found my way to the hospital chapel. As I sat in the half-dark stillness, with the cries of Rita's mother still echoing in my heart and the image of Paul's battered and motionless form still before my eyes, the full horror of what had happened suddenly closed in on me.

I've always had a fear of drowning, and when I closed my eyes there in the chapel, I saw an image of a wild and storm-tossed sea, about to swallow me up in its black turbulence. Drowning in a real ocean could not have been more agonizing. I felt as if I were being strangled and I wanted to scream out my pain, but I could hardly even breathe.

And then, from somewhere in the depths of that moment, I heard the words, "Peace, be still." The ocean of pain that was bearing down on me began, ever so slightly, to draw back as I grabbed hold of those words. They became a life raft for me, and I held onto them, repeating them again and again, until the waves of anguish started to subside and a deep inner stillness slowly, gradually, settled over me.

The words, of course, belong to Jesus. He spoke them to calm the raging sea (Mark 4:39). I don't know whether the sea image and the words came to me that night by way of my own unconcious mind or whether some burn-through of time reached me across the centuries, or whether they were a gift of the moment, a grace attesting to Christ's presence with me in my dark night. It doesn't matter. I do know that the experience was more real and more vivid than anything I could imagine or dream.

Many times in the days and nights that followed, that sea of emotion came back, again threatening to drown me; and each time it did, I closed my eyes and listened until I began to hear, once more, those calming, reassuring, life-saving words: "Peace, be still. Peace, be still. Peace, be still." Again and again they proved to be my life raft. They did not take me away from reality. I was always very much aware of the terrible thing that had happened, but at the same time I was also very much aware of something strong and solid and sustaining that *would not let me sink*. I could not have stood the anguish of that time without it. So I *know* that meditation (because that's what my repeating of Christ's words was) helps me to maintain my link with God. I *know* that it is not just a mind-trick or a crutch that will break under stress. I now have a deep inner certainty that there is *nothing* that could happen to me that I could not endure.

Paul did recover and is now putting his life back together. Of course, he has to live with the memory of the tragedy and it hasn't been easy, but he, too, has learned to touch the sustaining power of Christ through meditation. He's going to make it.

Since that December night, the storm-tossed sea has become a symbol, for me, of emotional upheaval. (I have since discovered that the image is used similarly by others, so it may be archetypal.) That is why I have written the following meditation for you. I hope it will help you to find your way to shore sometime when you are swept up in the raging currents of emotion.

Guided meditation number 10: the storm-tossed sea

Try to find a place where you can be alone, even if it's only for a few minutes. Then close your eyes and begin to visualize a violently stormy sea. Imagine that the whole scene takes place right in the center of your chest. Ugly, threatening breakers swirl and leap high in the air, then crash against sharp, jagged rocks.

Name the storm after the emotion you're feeling. For instance, "This hurricane is the anger I feel toward Fred." Then pour all the energy of the emotion into those waves and watch them crashing against the rocks with hurricane force. Feel it. Feel it. Feel it. ☐

Now begin to listen, above the waves, for the stilling words. It may help to visualize the figure of Jesus reflected in the sky above the storm, holding up His hand and saying, "Peace, be still." ☐

When you have heard the words, begin to repeat them to yourself, all the time keeping your attention on the water. ☐

Then see the whole scene gradually quieting. Let the waves begin to smooth out, the deafening noise subside. Deliberately calm out your sea until only the slightest ripple remains on its placid surface. ☐

Rest in that quiet, soothing mind-space for as long as you wish, continuing to repeat the words, "Peace, be still."

Jesus, man of quiet power whom even the winds and sea obey, thank You for Your firm command that stills my inner storms. Amen.

8

Meditation brings order into daily life

YESTERDAY morning, my ironing was interrupted by a telephone call, and when I returned to the task, my mind was still on the phone conversation. I ran the iron over half a shirt before I realized that the wrinkles were not smoothing out, in spite of my efforts. Of course I discovered, then, that I'd forgotten to plug the iron back in.

How many times over the years I've tried to smooth out the wrinkles in my life without plugging in to the Power Source! How many times I have made up my mind to get organized, improve my housekeeping, be more efficient, and then slipped right back into the old habits despite my good intentions. And all because of the mistaken notion that I could impose order on my life from without. Impossible. It just cannot be done. A clock whose inner workings are out of

168

synchronism can't keep good time, even with a perfect crystal, face, hands, and case. More and more, I am coming to realize that, when my inner self is in order, my outer life just automatically reflects that orderliness.

Don't get me wrong. I'm still not perfectly organized and my house is far from spotless, but I've found that even on the busiest days, if I just take time to meditate, I accomplish more and with less effort because of the *internal ordering* that occurs during my quiet time with God.

This internal ordering serves as a protective shield against external disturbances.

Something similar to this happens in the physical world. It's called the *Meissner effect*. When certain metals and alloys are placed in magnetic fields and then cooled to a sufficiently low temperature, an interesting thing happens. The electrons, which have been in a state of disordered random motion, enter into an *ordered state*.

Like those electrons in their state of random motion, most of us are so strongly influenced by forces outside of ourselves that our energies are constantly scattered.

Because of this, we use up tremendous amounts of energy to accomplish very little. But when we withdraw our energies from the external world through meditation, we "cool down" that inner agitation and our minds become serene, uncluttered, orderly. If we do this regularly, over a period of time this "cooled out" state will carry over into our daily lives, providing us with a valuable degree of immunity from disrupting external influences.

Roy Eugene Davis writes, in his book *Darshan: Vision of Light*, "When one meditates regularly there is, in time, a *meditative mood* which pervades the consciousness at all times so that whenever there is an occasion, when the mind is not occupied with matters of the day, the attention naturally turns within to contemplate the truths of life."

There are some very specific things you can do to stimulate that meditative mood and the ordered life that results from it.

Check your priorities

The first and most obvious one is to rearrange your priorities so that meditation is the one thing in the day that you absolutely will not let yourself skip, no matter what else comes up. This is a little scary at first. On a packed-full day, I have often thought, "I just don't have *time* to meditate today." But I've learned that those are exactly the days when I need it the most. When Rex and I were first married, I had trouble dividing my time between the housework and the yard work, but I soon learned that, if I'd get my inside work done *first*, then the outside tasks seemed easier to do. Meditation is the "inside work" that orders the events of our day.

As William Johnston notes, in *Silent Music*, "Some scientists are open to the hypothesis that in meditation a life-force is released which is more significant than nuclear energy." I don't know whether this is the case or not. I do know that when I begin my day with meditation, I don't bog down by midafternoon; I don't huff and puff up the basement stairs; I don't feel so overwhelmed by big tasks, such as a three-week stack of ironing to do or all twenty-two windows to wash. It's because then I'm plugged into the Power Source whose supply of energy is never depleted.

Here's something to try, especially on those busiest days.

Morning meditation for a busy day

As soon as you wake up in the morning, while you're still lying in bed, mentally run through the things you plan to get done that day. Then visualize yourself doing each task in SLOW MOTION. When I suggested this to my meditation class, one young man said, "But I'd get fired!" Well, I don't expect you to actually *do* the work in slow motion, but just visualize it that way before you begin the day. It somehow smooths out the tangles in your mind so that you can glide through your work with less friction. Obviously, you don't need to visualize each task all the way to completion. Just picture yourself doing it in slow motion long enough to get that graceful, slow-and-easy *feel* connected with the task planted in your mind. The same easy feeling is likely to come back when you are actually doing the work.

Then . . . get up, sit in a chair, close your eyes, and meditate, using the Logos,

"He that is within me performs the thing that is appointed for me" (Job 23:14). If you get a late start and absolutely can't take time for a sitting meditation, use the above Logos as you are getting dressed, while you're brushing your teeth, eating breakfast and performing your usual early-morning routine. Repeat it mentally on your way to work and/or *while* you are working. Let Him do the work *through you*, one job at a time. You will be surprised, if you persist in this working meditation, that this is exactly what happens. Some days, when I have meditated my way through my work, I look back on the accomplishments of the day and it hardly seems that I have worked at all, and yet my list is all checked off. You may find that hard to believe until you've actually experienced it. The only proof I offer is what you will provide yourself, when you put it into effect.

Part of the secret lies in abandoning yourself to the will of God, leaving it all up to Him.

Let God do it for you

My father used a formula to teach me how to bowl. It was: "Pick a spot in line with the center pin, aim your whole self toward it, and then *let go of the ball*." There's a definite parallel between my father's bowling formula and creative, successful achievement in any line of work. Artists, composers, writers, inventors—all creative people use the same formula, and the most important of all that formula is the last part: *let go of the ball.*

Thomas Merton, the brilliant and talented Trappist monk and extraordinary writer of our century, told of his spiritual odyssey in *The Seven Storey Mountain*. He wrote:

> . . . Sometimes I would be preoccupied with problems that seemed to be difficult and seemed to be great, and yet when it was all over the answers that I worked out did not seem to matter much anyway, because all the while, beyond my range of vision and comprehension, God had silently and imperceptibly worked the whole thing out for me, and had

presented me with a solution. To say it better, He had worked the solution into the very tissue of my own life and substance and existence by the wise incomprehensible weaving of His Providence.

But you don't have to be a monk or live in a monastery to order your life according to the will of God. Regular daily meditation is like a sailboat. If you do your part by raising the sail, the winds of God's grace will fill it and so propel you across even the most turbulent waters.

Learn to carry your own peace

I think it was Erma Bombeck whose kids said, "Mom belongs to the peace-and-quiet generation." Well, I guess I fit in that group, too. Trouble is, I never seem to find enough of it. If the TV isn't blaring, the record player is, or else there's a wrestling match on the family room floor, or the phone is ringing or the dogs are barking or there is a group of teen-agers dancing in the basement or eating pizza in the kitchen.

I learned, quite a few years ago, that if I was going to have any peace at all, I'd just have to carry it within me.

Now I know you can't be meditating all the time (although there *are* some advanced souls who are able to maintain a meditative state all the time). Until you and I become that adept, though, here is a way to induce that same relaxed, ordered feeling periodically during the day.

At the end of each regular meditation period, sit quietly, with eyes still closed, and try to *memorize* the peaceful feelings that are coursing through your body and mind. Notice the heaviness in your legs, the soft, rhythmic nature of your breathing, the glow that seems to surround you, the emotional equilibrium you feel. Sometimes during meditation you'll experience a profound feeling of freedom, or an inner playfulness, or a floating sensation. *Notice* these mental states and any images that may accompany them (such as dancing on the clouds, drifting on water, or riding on a ray of light) and try to memorize them. Then, as you go about your daily activities, stop occasionally (if not physically, at least mentally) and remember those sensations in detail. It may help to form a picture in your mind of yourself sitting quietly in your favorite chair, with your eyes closed in meditation. If you'll get in the habit of doing this several times during the day, you'll be surprised at how relaxed and in control you'll feel, how centered and internally ordered you'll be. All of this will reflect in your work, reducing fatigue, renewing, ordering your days. You'll begin to pay less attention to irrelevant things; you'll be less distractable, more *together*.

Symbols help establish internal order

Another aid that can help you to order the external activities of your life by first establishing inner orderliness is the *symbol*. Words are symbols. For instance, the word *God* is a symbol for the living reality it represents. Shapes can be symbols, too. The cross, for instance, is a symbol for Christ or for Christianity. When we use the word *God* in prayer, or when we place a cross on the altar of our church, we all realize that we are not worshipping the *word* God or the *shape* of the cross, but the reality behind these symbols. With this in mind, symbols can be a real help to us in *establishing contact* with that reality. For example, if I asked you to meditate on your relationship with God, it would be difficult to do so without going into a discursive meditation—in other words, thinking in words. There is certainly a time and place for this type of meditation, but it would not help with internal ordering of consciousness. However, if I were to draw a large circle and place a dot in the center of it and ask you to meditate on the circle as a *symbol* of God and tell you that the dot represents you, you would then have something tangible to focus on. Through it you could *experience* your inseparability from God, His omniscience and omnipresence, His eternal, unchanging nature, and much more. The ordered perfection of the form could be absorbed into the deeper levels of your consciousness, where it could serve as a lens through which your world is brought into focus.

Since we are talking about establishing orderliness within, let's look at what a psychiatrist, Dr. Roberto Assagioli, has to say about the use of symbols in meditation:

> Symbols can be visualized and this sets into motion unconscious psychological processes. This is an effective means for the transformation of the unconscious.

For the purpose of trying out the technique, let's work with two basic symbols: the cross and the circle. You may want to combine the two or meditate on them separately. I would suggest that you *draw* your symbol on a piece of paper or cardboard instead of using a design that someone else has made. I think it will be more meaningful to you that way. You may draw just a simple cross with a black felt-tip marker, or maybe you'll decide to use colors. You might choose to center the cross inside of the circle, or to draw a circle at the intersection of the lines of the cross, or to combine the two in some other way. If you feel inclined to embellish your design with additional lines and colors, go ahead, but make sure that the circle and the cross remain the dominant forms. Also, be sure to keep your design symmetrical. When I use this form of meditation, I usually feel more comfortable with a simple design, but once in a while I seem to be in a rather complex mood and then I enjoy drawing more elaborate designs. You may want to use the same design over and over, or you might enjoy drawing a new one each day. C. G. Jung, who was not only a psychiatrist but also a deeply religious man, made it a practice to draw a circular design in his notebook every day and then to meditate upon it. He wrote, "The circular image represents the wholeness of the psychic ground or to put it in mystic terms, the divinity incarnate in man."

After you have drawn a symbol, using the cross and the circle, study it for a few minutes. What is the general *feeling* generated in you by the design? Does it stir any particular emotions? Do parts of it remind you of some object in nature or some man-made thing? Does the way in which you have combined the two symbols suggest to you any deeper meanings about your relationship to Christ? To God the Father? To the Holy Spirit? Do you like the *feel* of the symbol? Write down your reactions to the design. This can be especially revealing if you draw different ones on different days.

When you have completed the above procedure, focus your eyes on the symbol for one minute. Then close your eyes and see it with your inner eyes—your spiritual eyes. Keep your attention centered on the symbol, assimilating its symmetry into your being. If thoughts distract you, as soon as you realize that your attention has strayed, calmly and easily "feed" the thought into the symbol and let it be absorbed into it. This is the symbolic equivalent to the prayer of relinquishment, in which you turn everything over to God. Continue to meditate in this way for fifteen or twenty minutes, and you will emerge from your meditation with an eagerness to do whatever needs to be done during the day. I often feel led, after this type of meditation, to make a list of my tasks for the day or the week, and I am always astonished at how there seems to be a perfect niche for each job, with time left over. The feeling of internal orderliness can be replenished any time during the day by centering the attention again on the symbol you have drawn.

Here is a guided meditation that will help you get centered.

Guided meditation number 11: you in the circle

1. Take a piece of string about twenty feet long. Tie the ends together and then lay it out on the floor in a circle. Stand back and look at the circle and feel its *wholeness*, its essential unity. Very soon, you will become a part of that oneness.

2. Imagine that, extending upward from the floor and following the outline of the circle is a cylindrical wall of light, representing the brightness and purity of Christ. You are about to step into that Holy Presence. Before you enter, ask God's blessing on your meditation. ☐

3. Then step to the center of the circle. ☐

4. Close your eyes and inhale a deep breath, drawing into you the invisible light of Christ. ☐

5. Spread out your arms so that your body

forms the shape of a cross, rising up out of the very center point of the circle. Imagine that you are suspended by the center of your head and that your feet are a firm and solid base. Your spine forms a perfect plumb line. Hold this position for a short time, feeling the balance and stability of it. ☐

6. Now lie down on your back within the circle. ☐

7. Place the fingers of one hand on a pulse spot, either in the neck or wrist. Use your pulse beat to adjust your breathing to a natural, steady rhythm in the following way: inhale deeply as you count four pulse beats; hold for a count of two more; exhale deeply to a count of four, and count two pulse beats before inhaling again. Continue in this way and in less than three minutes you will experience a feeling of peace and tranquility. ☐

8. With deepest love and devotion, dedicate the work of the day to the Lord. Ask Him to work in and through you during the whole day, giving you wisdom,

guidance, strength, and especially a loving heart. *Trust* Him to do it. ☐

9. Rise to a sitting position and then a standing position, staying as close to the center of the circle as possible. Once more, extend your arms and feel the balance of the cross rising from the center of the circle. ☐

10. Step out, pick up the string, and begin your day in the sure, steady awareness of the perfection of the pattern of all creation, reflected within you.

Frank Laubach, whose "each-one-teach-one" method brought literacy to 6 million persons, wrote this about his constant attempt to keep himself centered in God:

This concentration upon God is *strenuous*, but everything else has ceased to be so. I think more clearly. I forget less frequently. Things which I did with a strain before, I now do easily and with no effort whatever. I worry about nothing, and lose no sleep. I walk on air a good part of the time. Even the mirror reveals a new light in my eyes and face. I no longer feel in a hurry about anything.

Everything goes right. Each minute I meet calmly as though it were not important. Nothing can go wrong excepting one thing. That is that God *may slip from my mind* if I do not keep on my guard. If He is there, the universe is with me. My task is simple and clear.

Help me to keep my soul centered in You, Lord, all through this day. If I can do that, the universe will be with me. Amen.

9

Living in the divine flow

To the One Who Said, "I Am the Way"

Your Way is like a river, Lord,
its veiled and timeless Source
reaching back before beginnings
and down the steep and winding years,
   calling, calling, calling . . .

Above the noisy neon crowd,
within the catacombs of mind,
Your singing spring of Living Water
pursues me, ripples through me,
   calling, calling, calling . . .

A gentle mountain stream,
nudging, leading, never forcing,
a rush of joy, a breathless hush,
and the whispered brush of Love,
   calling, calling, calling . . .

I crack Your pure and crystal grace

on jagged rocks of sin,
then You, Son of Man, River, God
  within,
become a silvered waterfall, still
  calling, calling, calling . . .

The part of me that's river, too . . .
restless, churning, swirling, yearning
  . . .
echoes back Your haunting call.
Gather in my errant waters, Lord;
sweep me up in homing tides.
Make my way Your Way, blessed
  River;
Return my soul to the Cosmic Sea.

I did not intend to start this chapter with
a poem. I prepared for the writing of the
chapter in my usual way—reading,
gathering quotations, consulting my
spiritual journal, praying, dedicating it to
Christ, and finally, meditating before I
began writing. Then, when I put pen to
paper, the poem, above, just seemed to flow
out onto the page. Why am I giving you
this behind-the-scenes report? Because that
writing experience illustrates exactly what
this chapter is about. There is Something

in the universe—call it what you will—(the Way, cosmic flow, divine plan, will of God) that, *totally beyond the laws of chance or coincidence*, directs the lives of those who are in tune with it. *If you can position yourself in the flow of that force*, you will find that, more and more, you just happen to be at the right place at the right time; you manage to find the right words to say what needs to be said; you find yourself doing the kind of work you enjoy and do best; and when you have a need, the right person or thing just happens (?) to come along to fill that need. Almost everyone has had an experience or two like this, and most often, such events are chalked up to coincidence. But when one is really "in the divine flow" they become the rule rather than the exception.

But *how* do you tune in to that force? The answer is: by making an offering of *yourself*. You have to plunge, naked, into the great Flow and let It (which is, of course, God-in-action) carry you where and how It will. Is that scary? It shouldn't be. It is the Perfect Pattern, and within it, all things really do "work together for good to them that love the Lord" (Romans 8:28).

Will you lose your individuality? No. You will find out who you *really* are. William Johnston said it beautifully: "When I am most united with God, I am most myself."

The secret

But why is it that some people, even some who are good Christians and who pray fervently, can't seem to make Romans 8:28 work in their lives, while for a few others it seems so easy and natural? The answer is in the fact that the *vehicle* by which the Way is made known to man—the line that connects the individual soul with the Great Pattern—is the *unconscious mind*. You may "say prayers" all day, but if it's all done on a purely cerebral level—in other words, if the door to the unconscious is closed, it's going to be nearly impossible for the perfect spiritual answer to get through to you. It's like talking into a phone that's been disconnected. If you're going to receive guidance, if you're going to learn to flow with the River, you're going to have to learn to *open up the connection between your conscious and unconscious mind*. That's the

189

great secret. It's the door you have to open. "Knock and it shall be opened unto you" (Luke 11:9).

How do you knock? There are some very specific things you can do to open up that connection between your conscious and unconscious mind and to keep it clear. Just the act of meditation itself will greatly increase your ability to tune in to the cosmic Flow, because the meditative state is one in which there is a free and easy interplay between the conscious and unconscious minds. When you get in the habit of meditating regularly, you will often find yourself, at other times during the day, thinking of someone you haven't seen for a long time and then getting a letter or phone call from that person, or getting a creative idea "out of the blue" for a project or activity, or feeling led to look in a certain place for a lost item. If you will pay attention to these inner leadings and *follow through on them, you will soon come to know* (experience firsthand) what it means to be "in the flow of the divine plan."

In addition to your regular daily meditation, there are some other things you can do to keep the door open.

First, *pay attention to your dreams.* Many of them are post cards to you from your inner self (small *s*), and some of them are undoubtedly messages from the great universal Self (capital *S*). Psychiatrist C. G. Jung calls this the "collective unconscious," and notes that through it "we receive information that cannot be reduced to experiences in the individual's past." I believe that this is one of the channels through which God directs our lives. He did this all the time in biblical times. Why not now? Because we are too sophisticated to listen to our dreams. We must truly become as little children if we are to knock on that door that is waiting to open for us.

The other day, I was trying to get a message through to my friend Betty. I'd called several times during the day and again in the evening, but I kept getting the busy signal. Since the message was important, I called back later that night and, as it turned out, I got my friend out of bed. God sometimes has to wait until we've dropped off to sleep to get a clear connection to send His messages through to us, too. That's why it's so important to pay attention to our dreams. A thorough discussion of dreams would be a bit beyond the scope of this book, but I will give you a few suggestions that may help you tune in to them. Here are some prods that may help you to remember your dreams.

1. Read a good book about dreams, such as *Creative Dreaming*, by Patricia Garfield. Besides giving you suggestions for remembering your dreams, just reading such books will focus your attention on your own dream life, and you'll find yourself remembering them.

2. Just before going to sleep, tell yourself that you are going to remember a dream when you wake up. Then put your wrist watch or ring on the wrong arm or finger, or do something else that will catch your attention as soon as you wake up. This will remind you to try to recall your dream before you get out of bed.

3. Keep pen and paper on your bedside table and get in the habit of writing down your dreams in the morning. (Some people even do it in the middle of the night, but this takes more discipline than most of us have.)

4. If other family members are receptive, it's fun to share your dreams over

the breakfast table. In some cultures, this is a tradition. You'll be surprised at the correlations that will arise, and the subtle overall directing force it can be within the family. (The Way again!)

As you get more and more in tune with your inner self through your dreams, you'll become more adept at recognizing and interpreting the symbols, and you'll begin to see patterns emerging and meanings becoming clearer.

Since I've been paying attention to my dreams, I've noticed that often, when I have a decision to make, the symbols in my dreams will provide the answer I seek. For instance, when I decided to write this book, I debated with myself about whether or not to ask for time off from teaching in order to work on it. On the one hand, it would mean a loss of income and I might not be able to get my job back after I finished the book. On the other hand, I knew this would be the kind of book that could not be written in bits and pieces and sandwiched in between preparing lectures and grading essays. What should I do? One night, while I was still undecided, I dreamed that I was expecting a baby, and

I remember feeling a most incredible love for this dream child. I went happily around the house, getting out the crib and baby buggy and bathinette and baby clothes and carrying them upstairs in my dream. Then suddenly there I was standing in the middle of the living room with all that baby furniture and there was no place to put it. In fact, in my dream, the whole house was now suddenly crowded with all kinds of *junk* that seemed to be closing in on me. Then I looked in the crib and it was just *stacked full* of—guess what?—students' essays! I started grabbing up the papers and throwing them out the window, but I couldn't get rid of them. I'd throw out a bunch and more would come to take their place. I guess I woke up then. At least that's all I remember about the dream, but it was not hard to interpret. The "baby" I was so happy about was a symbol for this yet-unwritten book. The idea for the book had been conceived and was starting to grow within me, and I was trying to prepare a place for it in my life, but there was no room for it. When I looked closer to see what it was that was crowding it out, I saw the essays, which obviously represented my teaching job. In the dream, there was absolutely no question about which was more important, no problem in deciding what to do. The morning after that dream, I called the head of the English department at the college and asked to be temporarily relieved of my teaching duties. He was very nice about it and said, "Just remember we'll want you back next year."

When you first start trying to "read" your dream messages, you may wonder how to tell whether or not your interpretation is right. This really isn't much of a problem. As you get into it, you'll find that, when you hit the correct interpretation, it will just *feel* right. For me, it's kind of a "clicking in" sensation, a "perfect fit" between conscious and unconscious, an inner knowing that is almost tangible.

Twilight imagery

Closely related to dreams but even more exciting and revealing are the "twilight images" that come to us in that transition state of mind between waking and sleeping.

These are called hypnagogic images if they occur as you're falling asleep and hypnapompic if they happen as you're waking up. The terms aren't important, but the images themselves are fascinating!

I didn't know there was such a thing until one night, after I'd been meditating several years, the image of a bird suddenly flashed before my mind as I was falling asleep and then was gone. I remember thinking, "What was *that*?" Then, in the next second, I saw another bird, flying in the opposite direction. This disappeared and I saw a bird sitting on a tree branch, which was then replaced by a descending bird, and then an ascending one. The images seemed to come all by themselves. I was just a spectator. In fact, I became aware of them only after they were gone. I was absolutely enthralled with what had taken place.

Only a few days later, as if in answer to the questions the experience had stirred in me, I read about this phenomenon in a book by William Johnson, called *Silent Music*. I have since read about hypnagogic imagery in several other sources, and I have found that my ability to tune into these images increases as I continue to sharpen my awareness, through meditation. In addition to the visual images, *verbal* cues also come to me very frequently while I am in this state of consciousness. Words just seem to float across my mind. Sometimes they appear to be meaningless, but I write them down and often, later, I discover that they carry a symbolic meaning of importance to my life.

Dr. Elmer Green at the Meninnger Foundation in Kansas has done some fascinating research on hypnagogic imagery. His subjects report that these images "emerged full-blown, so to speak, without consciously being willed; vivid visions of people, scenes, objects, *known and unfamiliar* [italics mine] to the subject. And they were changeful, as if a very private showing of lantern slides were being run through the theatre of the mind."

Experiments such as Dr. Green's suggest that all people have access to these images from the collective unconscious but that most are not *aware* of them.

As I become more conscious of these images in my own mind, I have received guidance and direction from them. I believe that there is *spiritual significance* in this fact. As Johnston notes: "It is not at all uncommon for religious people to receive deep enlightenment in the twilight zone between waking and sleeping, or at some time in the night. For this is precisely the time when the conscious mind is open to receiving communications from the teeming womb of the unconscious."

This must have been the channel through which many of the visions of the Bible were transmitted. For instance, in Acts 16:9–10, we read, "And a vision appeared to Paul in the night; There stood a man of Macedonia, and prayed him, saying, Come over into Macedonia, and help us. And after he had seen the vision, immediately we endeavoured to go into Macedonia, assuredly gathering that the Lord had called us for to preach the gospel unto them."

This whole subject is so fascinating to me that I find myself wanting to tell you all about the various experiences I have had with hypnagogic imagery, but I'm afraid that would make another whole book, so by way of example, I'll just tell you about one. There was a time, several months ago, when I was considering a course of action that would have brought about a very crucial change in our family. I went to bed one night, intending to announce my decision to the family the next day. Just as I was drifting off to sleep, a vision appeared on my mind's "screen." It was of a broken picket fence, with several of the posts falling over. On one of the posts that was still standing, the letters H O L D flashed out at me with such brilliance that I was simply stunned. I could not have missed that message! I knew, in that moment, that my decision had been rash and that I should reconsider. How much pain and heartache that message saved our family! How glad I am that my receiving channel was open that night.

As I have become more and more attentive to these twilight images, I have learned some ways of opening myself to them. Maybe these techniques will help you to discover this marvelous inner reality —this part of the great cosmic ocean that every human being has access to.

How to increase receptivity to twilight imagery

1. There is a direct relationship between the *regularity* of my meditation and the amount and vividness of the twilight imagery I experience. Most of the images come to me, not while I'm meditating but as I'm falling asleep (though occasionally I have had some during meditation itself), but regular meditation seems to be the plow that prepares the ground for receiving the imagery seeds. So the first thing you can do to increase your chances of tuning in to the inner messages is to keep up with your regular meditation.

2. Also, the images are more likely to occur when you are not overly tired. The reason for this is that it seems to be necessary to maintain a certain level of consciousness in order to be able to *notice* the images. If you're too tired, you'll let go and fall asleep without becoming aware of the inner show. So try to arrange your schedule so you can go to bed before you get too worn out. Or, if you are lucky enough to have the chance for an afternoon

nap, this can be an optimum time for receiving images.

3. Before going to sleep, tell yourself that you expect to receive some images. Place writing materials on your bedside table for recording them. Later, after you have been receiving images for several weeks, you'll be able to ask for answers to specific questions or problems or to specify that you want images that pertain to a certain area of your life (job, family, social life, etc.). It's best not to try to do this at first, though. It might keep you from "letting go" enough to receive spontaneously. Just be open to whatever images or words may come. Don't try to control the direction of the inner flow.

Guided meditation number 12:
descending into the unconscious

Begin by getting comfortable in bed and doing a progressive relaxation exercise, such as that described in Chapter 3. □
Read through the guided meditation I am about to give you until you know the

sequence so you won't have to stop and refer to the book. ☐

Then visualize yourself either in an elevator ready to descend into an underground gold mine, or in a glass diving bubble preparing to explore the ocean depths. Whichever you choose, begin at ground level and say to yourself, "I am on level ten now, which is the surface of my mind, and I am ready to go down into the depths of myself. I am relaxed and comfortable." ☐

Then feel yourself being lowered slowly and easily to level nine. When you feel yourself there, say, "I am now on level nine. I am calm, relaxed. I have let go of all tension. I will go deeper and become more relaxed." ☐

Let the elevator or bubble lower you gradually and gently to level eight, and say, "I am now at level eight, deeply relaxed, calm, serene. I will go deeper and deeper." ☐

Continue in this way through levels seven, six, five, four, three, two, and one. The exact words you use are not important, as long as they carry the message of deeper and deeper relaxation. When you reach zero level, you will be at the bottom of the gold mine or on the ocean floor. ☐

Now, there is a white movie screen in front of you. Sit down in a soft chair facing the screen and just *let go*. Wait for a picture to appear. Do not *try* to make it happen. Do not "think up" something. Whatever appears will do so without any help from you. You don't have to do a thing but wait and watch the screen. You may find, as I often do, that the images begin before you ever get to the lowest level. That's OK. In fact, it's fine. Just relax and observe. ☐

On the other hand, you might have another kind of problem. You might fall asleep without becoming conscious of any images. Dr. Michael Samuels and Nancy Samuels, in *Seeing with the Mind's Eye*, suggest a remedy for this: "One such technique is for a person to bend his arm at the elbow, keeping his hand in the air; if he begins to go to sleep, his hand will drop and wake him."

There is so much more I'd like to say about twilight imagery and messages from the unconscious, but this is just one *part* of meditation, and we need to move along now. As with any other meditation technique, we have to be careful not to let the *method* become more important than the goal, which is always to *experience God*, to become Christ-conscious, Spirit-filled beings.

Keeping a spiritual journal

Another thing you can do to position yourself at the center of the divine Flow is to keep a spiritual journal. I have been doing this for a couple of years now, and I have found that it really *reinforces* the benefits of meditation and accelerates spiritual growth. Morton T. Kelsey, in *The Other Side of Silence*, writes:

> One of the best ways of starting the inner journey is to begin keeping a journal, and this is more necessary once the journey is underway. . . . A journal can reveal the implications of one's inner ex-

periences so that they can be translated into the outer creativity and loving action that is the completion of the inner way.

In addition, simply writing these experiences down shows that they are worth recording and that the venture inward is being taken seriously, and this opens a person to further growth and inner development. . . . For many people starting a journal is the religious turning point in their lives.

Here are some guidelines that will help to make your journal experience meaningful:

1. Allow yourself ten minutes or more, at the end of one of your daily meditation periods, for writing in your journal. *Schedule it into your day* so that you won't always be waiting until you have the time (and never finding it).

2. Be sure to date each entry. This will be important to you as you become more and more aware of the *pattern* of your unfolding life and the meaning it carries. It will also cause you to notice the gaps that will inevitably occur in your journal entries, and you will then begin to see how spiritual growth seems to parallel periods of

regularity in recording. One note of reassurance here. If you find that there are long lapses in your journal writing, don't get discouraged and give it all up. Sometimes, when I notice that it's been quite a while since I made an entry, I'm inclined to think: So many important things have happened since I last wrote that I couldn't possibly "catch up." If this happens to you, forget about "catching up" and just start with *now*. Even if you've let some grapes wither on the vine, don't let that keep you from picking the ones that are ripe *now*.

3. What should you record in your journal? Ron Bradrick, who taught a college course I took on the psychology of consciousness and meditation, said this about the journal work he assigned us: "Just begin writing. What you choose to pay attention to will arise." I found that this was true! You may want to begin this way and let your journal take you where it will. Still, you might feel more comfortable with something a little more structured to get your writing motor started. If so, here is a plan you might follow for the first fifteen days.

Structured journal plan

First Day—Make a list of the ten most significant events in your life, up to the present time. Limit yourself to ten, and write no more than one sentence to indicate the "gist" of each event.

Second Day—List ten people who have had a substantial influence on your life. They may be family members, friends, employers, employees, clergy, teachers, or others who have had either positive or negative influences in your life. They may be people you have relationships with at the present time, or figures from your past. They may not even be still living, but they must at least be people whose influence you are *still feeling* in some way.

Third Day—Briefly describe three problems or decisions you are currently facing in your life. Do not take more than one paragraph to summarize each.

Fourth Day—List your goals in three columns as follows: Things I hope to accomplish . . .

this year   during the next ten years

Be brief. Write only a few words for each, just enough so you'll be able to identify them later.

Fifth Day—List, in one column, the things you like about yourself and, in another column, the things about yourself you'd like to change.

Sixth Day—Describe, in as few words as possible, the main tenets of your religious beliefs. *Do not* quote a creed of the Articles of Faith of your denomination, or any other prepared statement. Write only those things that *you* really believe, in your own heart and soul. If, in this soul-combing process, you come across some doubts, don't deny them or force them underground. My old aunt used to say, "Doubts can be the greatest faith-expanders in the world, *if we're not afraid to face them.*" She was right. Get them out from under the bed and down on paper. Then you can take them into meditation where God can help you to deal with them.

Seventh Day—Write down any questions you might have about life or death or any other subject that doesn't have pat, settled-once-and-for-all answers. To help you formulate your questions, imagine that you are going to meet a very wise Being who has access to all the knowledge and wisdom of the universe (because that is Who you *are* going to meet)! What would you ask such a Being?

Eighth Day—Look over your list of significant events and choose one that you'd like to explore further. Before you begin to meditate, think through the whole sequence of this past event. Recall as many of the details as you can. Consider the circumstances leading up to it and ask yourself in what ways it affected the course of your life. How would you change things if you were to relive that period? What emotions are stirred as you recall this event? After you have *thought* about the event for five or ten minutes, *leave off* discursive thinking and begin to meditate, using the technique you have found most effective for you. As you are meditating, thoughts and images relating to the event in question will probably occur. Just notice them and let them go. If the memories are painful, I'd recommend the *Divine Filter* meditation in Chapter 4. When you have finished your meditation (fifteen or twenty minutes), just write in your journal whatever you feel led to write. There may be new insights, questions, any number of things you'll want to write. The entry may be long or short, depending on your inner stirrings and also on the time available.

Ninth Day—Choose one person from your list of significant people. Write a brief summary of your relationship. How has it changed during the time you've known each other? Where does it seem to be going? If there are things you'd like to say to that person but couldn't say to his or her face, write these things in your journal. Now close your eyes and visualize that person; talk to him or her a little in your mind; if possible, imagine yourself climbing into his person and *being* that "other" for a few moments. Now, once again, give up verbal thinking and begin to meditate in your usual way. When you have finished meditating, record in your journal whatever seems to stand out in your mind regarding this experience.

Tenth Day—Choose one of the problems or decisions you wrote about on the third day. If it's a problem, write out all its ramifications as you see them at the present moment. List possible solutions. If it's a decision, list the pros and cons on both sides. No matter how much you've mentally batted around a problem or decision, getting it down on paper almost always improves your perspective and brings new insights. NOW—the most important part of this activity—*open your mind and heart* and accept the possibility that there may be an answer or solution totally beyond anything you have so far thought of. Free youself for a *creative leap* that may help you crash through the limiting perceptions of your rational mind to discover God's perfect resolution for you in this situation. In other words, *let yourself drift with the divine Flow* as you meditate. When your meditation period is finished, write down any ideas that may have come to you, no matter how ridiculous or irrational they may seem. Then close your journal immediately and put all thoughts about the problem or decision away until the next day.

Eleventh Day—Reread yesterday's entry and add it to any related ideas you may have had in the meantime. Follow the same meditation and journal procedure you used yesterday. Continue to do this each day until you feel, in the depths of your being, that you have found the right answer.

Twelfth Day—Choose one of the goals you listed on the fourth day and explore it in writing. Why is this aim important to you? What will you gain by accomplishing it? Does it conflict with any of your other goals? If so, which is more important? What steps do you plan for accomplishing the goal? When will you take the next step? Write out your answers to these and any related questions that may arise in your mind.

Thirteenth Day—Select one item from your list of personal assets and one from the list of your faults (fifth day). Write down all the things you might do to *enhance* the positive characteristic you have selected and to minimize or eliminate the fault. It may be that you will decide that the fault isn't serious enough to make an effort to change it. In that case, *accept* this trait as part of yourself and cross it off your list of liabilities. Now, as you meditate, focus your attention either on that quality you like about yourself or visualize yourself the way you will be when you have *eliminated* the fault.

Fourteenth Day—Before writing, today, use the Being of Light meditation in Chapter 2. When you have finished the meditation, sit quietly, experiencing the presence of Christ. Then write a "letter" to Him, telling Him how you feel about Him. Write it as you would write to a friend. You don't need a bunch of Thees and Thous or other reflections of biblical language. Be yourself. He knows and loves you the way you are. You will find that putting your feelings of devotion into writing causes them to expand, filling your soul with waves and waves of blessing.

Fifteenth Day—Choose a question from your list for the seventh day; then close your eyes and allow yourself to "see" Christ with your spiritual eyes. Greet Him, kneel before Him in your mind if that feels right, or sit at His feet, and ask Him your question. Then wait expectantly in His presence. Write down any thoughts or images that go through your mind, even if they have nothing to do with the question you asked or even if they seem to make no sense at all. More often than not, these answers come in symbolic form. After a few minutes, let go of the question and meditate in your usual way, making no further attempt to find the answer at this time. God gives us as much of truth as we are ready to hear at any given time. If we do not receive an answer, it is probably because we would not yet be able to understand it. Still, it is very important to keep asking the questions. Now that you have asked the question in earnest, the Lord will begin to make you ready for receiving the answer. That answer might break in upon your consciousness later in the day, or two weeks from now, or in ten years. It will come when you are ready for it.

You may continue to follow this structured plan for writing in your journal for as long as you wish, because you already have a wealth of material on which to build —those lists you made during the first week. Once your journal writing gathers momentum, you may just want to record your meditation experiences as they occur, letting your inner voice guide you.

I've already mentioned writing down your dreams and the twilight images that come to you. This is helpful in several ways. First, it focuses your attention on these events of your unconscious mind and thereby encourages you to bring them into consciousness; second, it preserves them so that, even if their meaning is not immediately clear to you, you can go back later and get fresh insights; and finally, it provides an *ongoing record* of the inner movement of your life. I would suggest setting off a separate section of your journal for dreams and images.

Don't shy away from recording your deepest emotions in your journal. When you're angry or upset or fearful or worried, it helps tremendously to get your feelings down on paper. It dissipates all that negative energy that is churning around inside of you, freeing you for more worthwhile things. Edward Fischer, in an article for *Worship* magazine, entitled "The Journal as Worship," wrote:

> Martin Luther found that to rage against his enemies helped him to pray better. If you must rage, a journal is a safe place to do it. If the spent anger leaves more space in the heart for prayer, that alone is a good reason for keeping a journal.

Well, this has been a long chapter that has chosen its own course. It departed completely from the outline I made for it, refused to let me work in most of the quotations I had intended to use, and finally went on longer than I thought it should. I think a short guided meditation is in order.

Guided meditation number 13: the river

Close your eyes, breathe deeply, and relax. ☐

Now imagine that you are walking in a dry and sandy desert. The sun is beating down on your back and the hot sand burns your bare feet as you trudge along, tired and thirsty. Put yourself *in* the scene and allow yourself to feel the discomfort for a minute or two. ☐

There is a high sand dune ahead and you force yourself to climb it. As you struggle to the top and look over it, you see a row of green trees, several yards away, going crosswise to the direction you face. You know this means water and you rush toward the line of trees. You can hear the water rippling now and you know it's a river. Keep going. Keep going. ☐

Now you stand at the edge of the beautiful, clear, singing River. Reach down and scoop up some of the Living Water in your hands and drink from it. As you do, you will feel a fresh, tingling sensation rippling through you. ☐

The Living Water has a magical effect on you, and now your only desire is to become part of the River, to merge into it and flow with it. There is a rubber raft waiting there for you. Climb onto it, lie back, and relax, letting go of all striving, all struggle, all tension. You are safe, cared for, protected, directed. The One who carries you is both River and Helmsman. Let go. Trust. Flow. Hear His voice: "I am the Way . . ." ☐

Loving Lord, let me flow with You. Through the mountains and the deserts of my life, be my well of sparkling water, springing up into everlasting life. Amen.

10

Group meditation

IT'S a beautiful green and gold morning. A soft wind ripples the prairie grass outside the window of my little home office. A blessed stillness has settled over the house after the rush of getting the family off to work and to school. Peace wraps around me like a blanket. As I sit here this morning, writing the last chapter in my book for you, we are surrounded by a circle of love. I have talked to the members of my meditation group and they have promised to send out loving thoughts and blessings to all who read these pages. A loving thought is a living thing. Once it has been given life, it goes on forever, so as you read these words, please know that you are part of a spiritual network that surrounds and enfolds you with love in Christ's name.

Before we can talk about group meditation, I need to say something that will seem to be a contradiction of the whole subject, and it is this: meditation is a private thing between an individual and his God; the inner experience can never be fully shared; each person must meet Christ in the monastery of his inmost being, in the secret temple where no one else may enter. Even if we experience the presence of God while we are in a roomful of people, that God-experience still takes place privately, in our own inner sanctuary.

If that's so, then what's the point of getting together with others for group meditation? I like the way Thomas R. Kelly puts it in his book, *A Testament of Devotion*.

. . . As there is a mysterious many-ing of God, as He pours Himself forth into the universe, so there is a one-ing of those souls who find their way back to Him who is their home. . . . Two people, three people, ten people may be in living touch with one another through Him who underlies their separate lives. This is an astounding experience, which I can only describe but cannot explain in the language of science. But in vivid experience of divine fellowship it is there.

From birth till death, we need other people. Most of the time that we are on this journey through the world, we are putting out invisible feelers, trying to make some kind of meaningful contact with other human beings. Unfortunately, our antennas usually touch only the outer garments of those we come in contact with. The relationships we form are between one *personality* and another. This is fine as far as it goes, but it still leaves us yearning, on some inner level, for a deeper touching, a more soul-filling closeness.

Yet now and then during the journey, we are fortunate enough to meet other travelers with whom we can share the *inner* pilgrimage, and then the veils of personality become transparent, and soul touches soul. We cut through all of the external differences that separate us and we discover that *we are* the bleeding hands and thirsting lips, the pierced side and thorn-gouged forehead; *we are* the clothed-in-light, transfigured body of Christ; *we are*, collectively, Son of God, Son of Man, many-faceted manifestations of the One. *We are Love.*

So we come together with those who share our devotion to the sacred journey in order to experience more fully the *unity* that *we are*. In time, a certain *group consciousness* develops that supports the private, personal meditative efforts of each individual. The anonymous author of the spiritual classic, *The Way of a Pilgrim*, describes the supportive benefits of the group in these words:

> Spirit can give itself to spirit and act beneficially upon another and attract another to prayer, to attention. It can encourage him when he is despondent, turn him from vice, and arouse him to holy action. And so by helping each other they can become more devout, more energetic spiritually, more reverent.

Furthermore, a meditation group can be a radiating center, sending out light and love that will have a healing and cleansing influence in the world.

How to start a meditation group

Here are some answers to frequently asked questions about forming a group for meditation.

1. *How can I find other people to join with me in forming a meditation group?* The first thing to do is to pray about it and meditate about it. I am going to give you a very specific way of doing this. It is the most powerful form of petitioning prayer I know. There is nothing magical or mysterious about this form of meditative prayer. It is based on Jesus' promise that "What things soever ye desire, when ye pray, *believe that ye receive them*, and ye' shall have them" (Mark 11:24). Jesus did not mean this metaphorically. He meant it literally. The whole key lies in believing that we have *already* received the things we pray for. But how can we believe such a thing as that? We can believe it because *time* is an illusion. As T. S. Eliot puts it in "Burnt Norton": "Time past and time future . . . Point to one end, which is always present." This is very hard for us to understand because our minds are so used to thinking in a *linear* way, but it is

true, and realizing it will help you to *pray believing*. The trouble is that, even when we try to pray believing, doubts creep in, little prickly fears that our prayer may not be answered. We need something tangible to hook our belief to, and that is the principle behind what I'm about to suggest to you. Here is how to proceed.

1. Ask God to put you in contact with others who share your deep interest in spiritual growth through meditation. *Trust* Him to do so and wait *expectantly* for it to happen.

2. Meditate in this way: draw a large circle on a sheet of paper and let this represent *time*.

3. Now place yourself at any position on the circle by printing your initial through the line you have drawn. Then move along the circle and draw another, smaller circle, at another point on the circumference of the large one. This small circle represents the meditation group you have prayed for.

4. Accept the thing as *already done*. Time is only an illusion, anyway. As your diagram shows, the whole circle is there at once, and the same thing is true of time,

even though we can focus on only one segment of it at a given moment.

5. Now that you have asked God to help you find your group and have made a *symbolic acceptance* of your answered prayer, all you need to do is to continue to hold that acceptance in your soul. For the first five minutes of every meditation period, hold the symbolic representation of your answered prayer in you consciousness, always remembering that *it is already done*. The group is now established on the circle of time and you are moving along on that circle, so it cannot help but come into manifestation in your life. (You can use this form of meditative prayer with any petition that you are sure is in line with God's will.)

While you are waiting, let some very subtle cues go out from you that would go unnoticed by most people but that would be picked up by one who shares your quest. You might carry a book on meditation with you, or casually mention the subject in conversations with friends, at home, at church, or in other places. Don't dwell on it. Just mention it and see if there is any response.

Be open to *all* people. You never know

whom God might send you. For instance, a chance remark by a taxi driver started one lady in our group on the path to Christian meditation. The invisible power of the Lord will draw to you those who share your desire for holy fellowship; you need only be ready to receive.

Other frequently asked questions about group meditation include:

2. *Once we have found each other, how do we get the group started?* Someone has to take the initiative. Why not invite the group to your house to talk about it? At this time, you can discuss how often you want to get together (once a week is ideal), and find a time and place that suits all. You'll probably also want to discuss a little about what you will do together and how long your meetings will last, but be careful not to get *too* structured. Be loose and flexible so you can fly on the wings of Spirit.

3. *Who should be included in a group?* Only those people who are sincerely interested in spiritual growth through meditation. Do not, under any circumstances, try to *recruit* members. Those who are in earnest—those whom God sends—will be drawn to the group.

They will find out about it and come to you. As Joel Goldsmith notes in *The Art of Meditation:* "Much as all those who are interested in the deep things of the Spirit would like to include their friends and families as their companions along the Way, this is not always practicable."

4. *Do all of the members have to agree theologically?* No. There is only one God. We are all one in Christ. The spiritual consciousness we tap into in meditation rises above dogma, above differences in interpretation, above denomination. Agree to be tolerant of superficial differences so that, together, you may rejoice in the unity of His love.

5. *Do we need a leader?* Well, you need someone to take charge of necessary arrangements—logistical matters. In most groups, there will also be one person who has had more experience with meditation than the others, and that person will probably feel led to provide some gentle direction, always encouraging others to bring in ideas, and share what they've read and experienced. Don't have any elections or formalize your structure in any way.

6. *What about financial matters?*

Whatever you do, don't have dues! This is not a club. However, you may want to buy some tapes of guided meditations or of lectures about meditations, or of music for meditation, and then everyone can chip in as necessary. There shouldn't be any other expenses.

7. *Should our meetings follow any particular sequence?* It is helpful to have some kind of plan, at least when you first start meeting. Having some idea of what to expect will make participants feel more at ease. Just remember to stay flexible. In fact, make it a point to break away from your usual sequence now and then in order to avoid rigidity. In our group, we usually talk informally for a while, with each person feeling free to bring up meditation experiences he or she has had during the week, or to ask the opinion of the others about a personal problem that relates to the spiritual life. We share insights from books we may be reading or passages of scripture that have taken on new life through our meditation, or whatever related things may be on our minds. Then we often listen to a taped lecture by a spiritual leader, stopping the tape whenever we want to discuss the

speaker's ideas. Finally, invoking the presence of Christ in prayer, we begin our meditation period. Sometimes we move into meditation by listening to a guided meditation that has been recorded. At other times, we preface our meditation time with some relaxation exercises or some soothing music for calming and centering ourselves. After this, we meditate in silence, each one in his own way. No one calls time. Each person just quietly gets up and leaves when he is finished meditating. I realize that this may seem rather abrupt to you, and you may prefer to have someone close the meditation period for all, with a short oral prayer or benediction. I would urge you though, not to stay and visit after you've meditated. You want to be able to carry away with you that silver-white silence of the spirit that hovers over the group, and if you revert to small talk, it will fly away.

8. *Should we have a regular meeting place?* You may want to take turns at various members' houses, or there may be one member who finds it convenient for the group to come to his or her house all the time. A church parlor may be an ideal place, too, if the minister or priest is in

sympathy with what you are doing. Wherever you decide to meet, a nice thing to do at one of your first meetings is to have a room consecration. Ask someone to read the following poem, or have copies made so you can all read it in unison.

Room consecration

In this room
grows the tree of life
and from it come
the fruits of health and wholeness.

In this room
is the spring of living water
which drowns the cry of death
and drains its power.

In this room
echoes the heartbeat of love
and from it resound
acts of kindness,
words of understanding.

In this room

lies the hidden manna
which falls from heaven
and gives spiritual nourishment.

In this room
hangs the mirror of the soul
in which we see
what we truly are . . .
sons of the Most High.

In this room
is the throne of God
and from it come
power and dominion
to those present.

In this room
hangs the yoke of Christ
and with it comes
the strength
to bear all burdens.

In this room
dwells God,
the Father of us all.

Jim Rosemergy

9. *What about meditation for others?* When we meditate, our consciousness becomes an open channel through which the laser beam of spirit may pass. A laser is a ray of light that is not diffused but goes directly to where it is sent. Now and then, you will want to dedicate your group meditation to some specific person or cause. A member or a loved one may be ill or plagued with a problem or desiring guidance on a project, or you may feel a special need to send out blessings for world peace or some other universal cause. As long as there is nothing controversial about it, this is a beautiful thing to do. The old saying that "more things are wrought by prayer than this world dreams of" will take on new meaning for you. It isn't necessary to focus your attention on the person or situation during meditation or to pray in words during the silence. Just make a statement, before the meditation begins, that you want to dedicate this meditation to a special person or cause and name who or what it is. Then clear your minds and begin meditating in your usual manner. Your dedication will direct the spiritual power that you plug into while you meditate.

10. *Should the group do anything between meetings?* Of course, group meditation should *never* take the place of private meditation, and you will naturally continue with that during the week. In addition to this, you may want to plan for some *spiritual trysts.* A tryst is an agreement to meet at a certain time. What I am suggesting is an agreement to stop whatever you may be doing at an agreed-upon-time, just long enough to close your eyes, feel the presence of Christ within you, and then spiritually touch the other members of your meditation group. If your group wants to try this, select a time of day that you can all associate with something you do regularly. For example, at 8:45 in the morning, John and Bill are driving to work, Anne is doing the breakfast dishes, Mary Lou is sitting in a class, and Pat is driving the children to school. These are activities that they do at the same time every day, so this helps them to remember the tryst. Set a definite time and try it for a week. You'll probably forget sometimes, but if you keep at it, it will soon become a habit—one that will draw your group together like an invisible magnet.

11. *Are there some things we should avoid in our meditation group?* There are a few cautions you should talk a little about at one of your first meetings, just as a safeguard against possible difficulties later.

a. Don't get into theological arguments. It's fine to discuss differences and to share ideas, even if they aren't in agreement, but this is not the place for proving one person right and another wrong. Listen and discuss but don't argue.

b. As you grow in your ability to meditate, you will no doubt have some exciting inner experiences you'll want to share with one another. This is good, because one person's experience may be a seed planted in the consciousness of another person, and that seed may eventually bear abundant fruit. *Just remember not to compare your progress with that of anyone else.* Christ works in each soul according to its own inner pattern. Such phrases as "on a higher level" or "more mature spiritually" or "farther along on the path" have absolutely *no* meaning. In fact, to make such comparisons reveals a lack of understanding of what the journey is all about.

c. No one should ever feel any pressure to share experiences, lead guided meditations, or contribute to discussions. The greatest contribution each can make is his own presence there. Some of the quietest members may be making the greatest input to the spirit of the group.

d. This is definitely *not* the place for "encounter-group" tactics. Putting people on the spot, making them feel uncomfortable, or dishing out personal criticism in the guise of "helping them face their hang-ups" should be avoided at all times.

If you will go over this list as you begin, discussing the items together, it may help you to avoid some problems later.

I'll close this chapter with a guided meditation for your group. I'd suggest that one of the members tape-record it so that all of you can participate together. You may do this with any of the other guided meditations in this book as well. The reader should read slowly, pausing adequately at the indicated places, and allow for a period of silent meditation afterward. The group may then disperse in silence, each person leaving when he finishes his own meditation, or if you prefer, the reader may close with the prayer given at the end of the meditation or with one of his own choosing. In the latter case, fifteen to twenty minutes should be allowed between the end of the guided meditation and the prayer.

Before you start the guided meditation, it's a good idea to have everyone stand up and stretch, especially if you've been sitting for quite a while. It's also nice to lower the lights and have a candle glowing during your group meditation, if you wish.

Guided meditation number 14:
love and light

Reader: Christ is the true Light that lights every man that comes into the world. His light shines in this room. It is in the very air we breathe. It is the light of Love.

Close your eyes now and take a slow, deep breath. As you inhale, feel yourself being filled with the pure white light of

Love. As you exhale, envision a mist of shining light radiating out from you to the person on your *left*. ☐

Inhale again, filling yourself with the light of Love, and then exhale, extending that light to the person on your right. ☐

Once again, inhale the light of Love; then exhale, letting that precious light extend outward from you until it fills the whole room, warming, blessing, illuminating all the members of our group with the love of Christ. ☐

The light that lights every man that comes into the world is burned into every atom and every molecule of your body, but it shines in darkness and we do not comprehend it. It is possible to comprehend that light! But the only way it can become visible to us is for our blind eyes to be touched by Love. Light . . . is Love . . . is God.

So now, as we sit together in this room, let us begin to sense the vibration of the perfect light of Love in every fiber of our being. Begin by focusing all of your attention on your feet, and allow yourself to feel, very distinctly, the current that is being generated there by the inner light of Christ. Do this until you feel warmth or a tingling sensation in your feet. ☐

Now raise your consciousness, together with the radiation, into your legs and feel them being charged with light. ☐

Now let the light move up to fill the whole central portion of your body. Feel it warming every tissue of your heart. ☐

Let it spread out into your arms and hands. Let it dance off the ends of your fingertips. ☐

Now feel the light illuminating your throat and mouth so that the words that go forth out of your mouth will carry the light of Love. ☐

Feel the soft glow of Love filling your mind and shining from your eyes so that you may see the perfection that is in all things. ☐

Now let every pore in your body beam out that light which is Christ—and in that divine light and Love, know, at this moment, that we are one in Him. □

As we go through the activities of the coming week, Lord, help us to remember to pour out Love as light, while we work, interact with our families, sit in church, shop, walk along the street—in every place, let us be prisms through which the light of Christ passes, beaming forth the splendid colors of divine Love. Amen.

THE END

Large Print Inspirational Books from Walker

Would you like to be on our Large Print mailing list? Please send your name and address to:

B. Walker
Walker and Company
720 Fifth Avenue
New York, NY 10019

A Book of Hours

Elizabeth Yates

The Alphabet of Grace

Frederick Buechner

The Adventure of Spiritual Healing

Michael Drury

A Certain Life: Contemporary Meditations on the Way of Christ

Herbert O'Driscoll

A Gathering of Hope

Helen Hayes

Getting Through the Night: Finding Your Way After the Loss of a Loved One

Eugenia Price

Inner Healing: God's Great Assurance

Theodore Dobson

Instrument of Thy Peace

Alan Paton

The Irrational Season

Madeleine L'Engle

Jonathan Livingston Seagull

Richard Bach

Living Simply Through the Day

Tilden Edwards

The Power of Positive Thinking

Norman Vincent Peale

The Touch of the Earth

Jean Hersey

Gift From the Sea

Anne Morrow Lindbergh

A Grief Observed

C.S. Lewis

A Guide to Christian Meditation

Marilyn Morgan Helleberg

Up From Grief

Bernardine Kreis and Alice Pattie

Walking With Loneliness

Paula Ripple

The Way of the Wolf

Martin Bell

Who Will Deliver Us?

Paul Zahl

With Open Hands

Henri Nouwen

Words of Certitude

Pope John Paul II

Words to Love By

Mother Teresa

The Sacred Journey

Frederick Buechner

Something Beautiful for God

Malcolm Muggeridge

Strength to Love

Martin Luther King, Jr.

To God Be the Glory

Billy Graham and
Corrie Ten Boom